the PLUCK of the IRISH

10 Notre Dame sports figures who made a difference

By Jim Hayden

BACK STORY PUBLISHING, LLC
www.backstorypublishing.com

The Pluck of the Irish

10 Notre Dame sports figures who made a difference

by Jim Hayden

ISBN: 978-0-9993967-4-2
Library of Congress Control Number: 2018941354

Paperback editions printed in the United States of America. For information on quantity discounts or special editions to be used for educational programs, fundraising, premiums, or sales promotions, please inquire via electronic mail at *admin@BackStoryPublishing.com*, or write to Back Story Publishing, Post Office Box 2580, Rancho Mirage, California 92270 USA.

News media inquiries may be directed to
newsroom@BackStoryPublishing.com

Credits

Jim Hayden graduated from Notre Dame with a bachelor's in fine arts. He then earned an MBA at Central Michigan University. Some of the people in this book were his classmates. Jim worked in the advertising industry in New York and Los Angeles, where he was a Senior Partner and Creative Director at Ogilvy & Mather. He won numerous national and international creative awards. He is a longtime volunteer for the Braille Institute, broadcasting weekly news for the blind and reading disabled. He lives in Beverly Hills, California.

Designer: Stuart Funk
Back Story Publishing Editorial Director: Ellen Alperstein

www.BackStoryPublishing.com

CONTENTS

FOREWORD

MY FATHER, HARRY ORNEST

It was 1948. He was 25 years old, and at his job at the ice rink. He was a hockey referee in St. Louis, Missouri. In 1983, he owned the arena where he used to referee — 35 years earlier.

Harry Ornest is the only man in professional league sports ever to have done that. Harry Ornest was my father.

He was born in Canada. His parents were Jewish, and they had come from Poland to live in a free country. It wasn't easy for them. His dad worked in a grocery store, and didn't make much money. His mother barely spoke English. They raised four boys, and my dad, Harry, was the oldest.

The boys were expected to do well in school, but they also

ORNEST FAMILY

When he was 25, Harry Ornest was a hockey referee in St. Louis, Missouri. In 1983, he owned the St. Louis Blues of the National Hockey League, as well as its home ice, St. Louis Arena — the same rink where he once refereed.

had jobs from an early age. By the time he was 7 years old, Harry was delivering newspapers and selling programs at the local ice rink in Edmonton, Alberta. As a little kid, he had found two things he would love his whole life — reading and sports.

He was a good athlete who played professional baseball in his early 20s. But in the 1940s, no one got paid much for playing sports, so he also had a job in the concession stand, at Renfrew Park in Edmonton. And even though he was good at sports, he wasn't good enough to play at a higher level.

"At 17," he once said, "I was a prospect. At 22, I was a suspect."

Dad had good sense of humor, and he loved to laugh, even at himself.

He became a hockey referee and a baseball umpire, traveling around the United States — if he couldn't play, he made sure he wasn't far away from the game.

In 1952, he married my mother, Ruth. She was also from Canada. They lived in Edmonton for a few years, then moved to Vancouver before settling in Los Angeles in 1962. I'm the oldest of four children. From the 1950s to the 1970s, we grew up listening to Dad talk on the phone, trying to talk his rich friends into buying a sports team, and letting him run it. He knew he could take a struggling team, build it up, and make it successful — he had what they call "vision." He just didn't have the money. Yet.

To support the family, dad went into the vending machine business. But he never stopped trying to get into the business of sports.

In 1978, the Pacific Coast League was expanding. That's a Triple A minor baseball league where major league players sometimes get their start. The expansion teams weren't too expensive, and Dad finally made his dream come true — he bought not just one, but two professional sports teams, the Vancouver Canadians, and, for his brother Leo, the Portland Beavers, in Oregon.

We were all thrilled for our dad.

At the time, I was working as an editor's assistant at a Los Angeles news radio station. It was a low-level job, and when Dad invited me to work for him and the team in Vancouver, I accepted. I learned the business from the ground up. I started by selling hot dogs at the concession stand, and Dad soon gave me the title of assistant general manager.

For a lot of team owners, minor league baseball is a hobby. Not for my dad — it was his business, and he had to make a living from it. And just as he had known all those years ago, he *was* good at it. Three years after he founded the Vancouver Canadians, he sold the team for a profit. Now, he didn't need other people to buy him a team, he could buy it himself, and he loved making the deals.

In 1983, the St. Louis Blues of the National Hockey League were losing money, and the team's owners wanted to sell it. It was much more expensive than a minor league baseball team, but Dad found a way to buy it, and the arena.

He was excited. He was stressed out. He had a lot at stake, but he knew what he was doing. He turned that team around, and in 1986, sold it for a nice profit. Three years later, he did it again, buying, then selling the Toronto Argos of the Canadian Football League. He was a sports mogul!

Even though Dad owned the team, he liked to answer the office phone sometimes. He wanted to hear from fans, whether they had something nice to say, or if they complained. I remember one letter from a fan he had talked to who wrote to say how impressed he was that Dad had taken the time to listen. Dad sent him some free tickets.

Sometimes during games, Dad would sit with the fans in the cheaper seats. If he saw trash in the arena, he would pick it up and throw it away. When a player got hurt, he went to the locker room to make sure the guy was OK.

Dad always loved the people and the games as much as running the business. And he still loved to read about them. He read books and, especially, newspapers, sometimes as many as four a day. This was before the internet, and often, he would read the paper with a scissors in one hand, and a pen in the other. If he saw an article he thought would be of interest to a sports writer, a friend, his lawyer, us kids, he would cut it out and send it to us with a note. Many people got thick envelopes filled with Dad's newspaper clippings.

Dad was a fast typist, and would type his own letters. He cared about the English language, and using it properly was as important to him as the value of a dollar.

Harry Ornest died too young. He was 75. He never stopped dreaming of owning another sports team, and he worked hard all his life to make it happen. My brothers, sister, and I are very proud he was our dad. We miss him. We hope these stories of notable Notre Dame sports figures inspire you as much as our dad inspired us.

— *Laura Ornest, 2018*

MY FRIEND, HARRY ORNEST

People connect with Notre Dame in a thousand different ways. They know about the university from movies, newspapers, and websites. Even though Notre Dame is in the middle of the United States — in South Bend, Indiana — people all over the world have heard about the "Fighting Irish" of Notre Dame.

Notre Dame is a university with high academic standards. The name is French, for "Our Lady," which refers to the Virgin Mary. Notre Dame was founded in 1842 by French-speaking priests as a Catholic university. You have to be a very good student to go there. But most people know about it because of sports.

The mascot of Notre Dame is the leprechaun, and the sports teams' nickname is the Fighting Irish. Supposedly, that name came from Irishmen who came to the U.S. and fought for the Union in the Civil War.

Many people have heard about "winning one for the Gipper." Those words refer to George Gipp, who played football for Notre Dame 100 years ago. The words were spoken after he died, by his coach, Knute Rockne, another famous Notre Dame name. He wanted the team to remember Gipp's fighting spirit, his will to win.

Some people have heard about "Touchdown Jesus." That's a nickname for a mural that overlooks Notre Dame Stadium — it's 134 feet tall, and depicts Jesus holding his arms high in the air, like a football referee signaling a touchdown.

Harry Ornest didn't attend Notre Dame, nor did any of his children. Like most people, he knew about the school and the Fighting Irish through movies and, especially for Harry, by reading about them in the newspaper. Harry, who died in 1998, 20 years before this book was published, was Jewish, and he never went to college. But Harry knew Notre Dame better than a lot of people.

He knew Notre Dame because he loved sports, and because he loved to read about sports. For many years, he lived in Los Angeles, and was a friend of a sports writer for the Los Angeles Times, the biggest newspaper in the western U.S.

Harry loved newspapers. He loved the words, the stories, the little surprises you get reading a good newspaper sports story.

Several years after he died, his children — Laura, Mike, Cindy, and Maury — wanted to honor his memory by honoring what he loved. They formed a charity, and one of its programs was the Harry Ornest Internship. Every summer, for 10 years, the internship sent a student enrolled in a special program at Notre Dame — the John W. Gallivan Program in Journalism, Ethics and Democracy — to the Los Angeles Times. The student got to work in the sports department of the paper, and it was a very big deal.

Every one of those interns deserved that job. They all did

great work, whether they were writing about the Dodgers or dodgeball. After graduating from Notre Dame, some of those young people stayed in the newspaper business; some took other paths. And they all knew who Harry Ornest was, and what he stood for. They all knew that he, and his family, had given them a valuable gift in their Notre Dame education.

This book honors Harry Ornest in another way, a way we hope Harry would like.

These 10 stories are about people who are or were associated with Notre Dame and its sports community. Some of them are famous athletes — a quarterback who broke records, a running back who was a Vietnam war hero, a basketball star who pioneered race relations. There's a story about a hall-of-fame coach, a swimmer whose accident almost left her paralyzed, a broadcaster who wasn't good enough to play sports, but excels at describing them. There are stories about Pulitzer Prize-winning writers, who explained what happened on the playing field, and also why.

And to begin, is the story of a priest who made sure that everyone at Notre Dame was a good person as well as a good athlete, coach, or teacher; a leader who made a difference at his university, and all over the world.

Harry Ornest never knew any of the people in this book. But their stories, and this book, are dedicated to him. We honor and thank him and his family for their gifts to the University of Notre Dame.

— *Bill Dwyre, former sports writer, Los Angeles Times*

INTRODUCTION

SHAPING HISTORY

Father Theodore Hesburgh

In 1927, airplanes were fairly new, and a lot of people had never seen one in person. That was almost 100 years ago, when 10-year-old Ted Hesburgh was a kid in Syracuse, New York, with a lot of energy and imagination. He loved the idea of flying. He built model airplanes, and, in his mind, flew them to exotic places all over the world.

One day, a barnstormer came to town. In the 1920s, barnstormers were daredevils, they were pilots who did stunts in an open-cockpit airplane. The planes were powered by a propeller, because jet engines hadn't been invented. Barnstormers were like circus entertainers in the air, doing fancy tricks, and giving people rides.

Ted talked his parents into letting him go for a ride

UNIVERSITY OF NOTRE DAME

Father Theodore Hesburgh was president of the University of Notre Dame for 35 years. His influence was felt not only on campus, but throughout the United States.

with the barnstormer. The wind blew around his face as he looked up into an endless blue sky. He looked down, onto an endless world, a world even bigger than his imagination. He was thrilled! From his view in the heavens, Ted felt like he could do anything he wanted, now and forever.

It was as if someone — God? — was whispering, "Dream big. You are meant to do great things."

And he did. By the time Ted died in 2015, when he was 97 years old, he had seen and done more things than that little boy — or anyone — could have imagined. He had set high goals, he had found a way around whatever got in his way, and he had made a difference for people all over the world.

Theodore Hesburgh played many roles over his long life. He was most famous for being the president of the University of Notre Dame for 35 years, from 1952 to 1987. Before that, he had studied at the seminary at Notre Dame. A seminary is where you learn to be a religious leader, like a priest, minister, or rabbi. After seminary, he continued to study. He went to Rome, Italy, then to Washington, D.C. Then he returned to Notre Dame to teach moral theology at the university.

He was so good at learning, teaching, and showing students the value of curiosity, that his bosses — other priests — made him president of the university. He was only 35 years old.

When Father Hesburgh took the job at Notre Dame,

which is in South Bend, Indiana, the university was known mostly for its outstanding football team. That was fine, but it wasn't enough for Father Hesburgh — he believed that Notre Dame could be as excellent in academics as it was in sports. He believed that Notre Dame should offer opportunities for all kinds of students, not just white males who could throw a football, or shoot a basketball.

Today, largely thanks to Father Hesburgh, Notre Dame is one of America's best universities, whether its students are playing football or doing science experiments. Father Hesburgh represented the best qualities of the people who came before him at Notre Dame, and he set a high standard for those who came with and after him.

In addition to being president of a major university, Father Hesburgh became one of the world's best-known humanitarians. A humanitarian is someone who devotes his or her life to helping people become the best they can be, no matter where they come from, how much money they have, or how they look.

Theodore Hesburgh was a Catholic priest, an educator, and a champion of human rights. He was also complicated and demanding. He was fair and imperfect. He devoted his life to God, but sometimes he disappointed the Catholic Church. Sometimes he disappointed the people at the university who had hired him to teach. Over the years, many U.S. presidents asked for his advice on many different topics. Sometimes, they didn't like what he told them, because his advice caused trouble for the "establishment" — the people in power.

Change can be difficult, and Father Hesburgh saw the need for many things to change.

In the 1950s, America was a troubled country. In many parts of the U.S., people of color were treated badly. Often, they were not allowed to vote, or to attend some schools. They were not allowed to buy houses in some places, and in some places they couldn't use swimming pools and restrooms that white people used. In short, they didn't get the same justice that white people got.

In 1957, Father Hesburgh had been president of Notre Dame for five years. He had raised a lot of money for the school. He had begun to improve its academics, and had started building the first of 40 new buildings. One of them is the library that is named for him. The library is also famous for a mural called "The Word of Life," but most people call it "Touchdown Jesus," because it shows Christ, with his arms raised like a referee signaling a football touchdown. You can see it from Notre Dame Stadium, where the football team plays.

In 1954, U.S. President Dwight Eisenhower had asked Father Hesburgh to serve on the National Science Board. The U.S. president was happy with the result, so in 1957, he asked Father Hesburgh to serve on the U.S. Civil Rights Commission. That group was formed to give the president advice about how to help Americans who weren't white get the rights they were supposed to have as U.S. citizens, but for so long had been denied.

Some people thought that Father Hesburgh should

just do his job at Notre Dame, where things were fine and everybody was happy. But Father Hesburgh said his job was bigger than just being president of the university. He said "yes" to Eisenhower. When you are cozy, and you step out of that so-called "comfort zone" to help others, it can be a brave thing to do.

Here's why: The commission members often disagreed about how everyone in America could get justice. They met only in Washington, D.C., which Father Hesburgh thought was too far from most of the injustice. He said, "We have to go where the problems are," meaning the southern U.S.

The other members said that could be dangerous. But Father Hesburgh was very moving — he said going to the South was the right thing to do. He said that it was important to gather facts, and that anybody trying to make trouble wasn't going to get in the way.

Father Hesburgh talked them into going to Alabama, where some people did make trouble. Like others, Father Hesburgh got death threats from racists, who don't believe that all people are created equal. The racists said that things in America should stay the way they were.

But the commission was brave, and the members finally came together to write their recommendations. Their advice helped create the Civil Rights Bill of 1964. To this day, that law is the guiding light for justice for all Americans.

Some years later, Father Hesburgh was chairman of the U.S. Civil Rights Commission, and there were still challenges to equal justice in America. When he thought the work of the commission was being slowed down by U.S. President Nixon, Father Hesburgh said so. President Richard Nixon was not happy. He fired Father Hesburgh as president of the commission.

Even though he was punished for speaking out for justice, Father Hesburgh continued to fight for it. He was a supporter and friend of Dr. Martin Luther King Jr., who was a famous champion of civil rights who also got death threats for his work. Sadly, in 1968, those threats became real when he was killed by an assassin.

As Father Hesburgh was helping the country see how different people can come together to make a better nation, he was helping Notre Dame do the same thing. In 1972, it began to admit women students as well as men, and it also invited students from different backgrounds to be students. Sometimes, those changes were difficult.

Once, Father Hesburgh heard about trouble three roommates were having. He asked them to come to his office. Two guys came, and told him that there was no more trouble because their roommate had left school to go back home to Philadelphia.

"I wonder why," Father Hesburgh said. The students shrugged.

"I mean," Father Hesburgh continued, "it takes a lot of effort to get here, it takes a lot of money. Then he leaves after a few weeks. I wonder why."

"I don't think he fit in," one boy said.

"Yes, not right for here," the second boy agreed.

Father Hesburgh nodded. Then he said, "I wonder if it was because he was Jewish."

The boys squirmed.

Father Hesburgh reached into his desk for a textbook. "Or I wonder," he said, "if it was because of this." He put the book on the desk. It had belonged to the boy who left. Someone had drawn a swastika on the cover. A swastika was the symbol of Nazi Germany, which forced Jewish people into prison camps during World War II. Millions were killed. Swastikas are still symbols of hatred, racism, and sometimes violence.

The students were silent, and a little scared. Father Hesburgh looked them in the eye and said, "Maybe he left because you guys harassed and humiliated him, and he couldn't take it anymore."

Father Hesburgh was very angry. These boys needed a lesson in how to treat people who were different from them.

"I'll tell you what you can do," he told them. "You can go back to your room, pack, and leave this university now. Or, you can go to Philadelphia, find that boy, and apologize — to him, his mother and father, his brothers and sisters, uncles, aunts, his friends, his neighbors, and everyone else within sight, and bring him back here by Tuesday."

The boys protested, saying they didn't know where he lived, that they didn't have money to travel.

"I'm sure your parents will be happy to help," Father Hesburgh said. "Want me to call them?" The boys shook their heads in terror. "Tuesday," he repeated, "and I may reconsider whether you stand for the same things this place stands for. Whether you fit in. If you don't go and apologize, you can pack your bags."

By Tuesday, all three students were back on campus, and back as roommates. It might have been the best lesson those boys ever learned at Notre Dame.

Even after Father Hesburgh became a famous educator and civil rights leader, sometimes he was still the little boy who loved to fly. With the help of the U.S. military, he got to ride in a fighter plane that took off from an aircraft carrier. He got to fly in and out of a volcano. But he really wanted to ride in the supersonic SR-71 spy plane, which could go 2,000 miles per hour. That was a big ask — the SR-71 was a big military secret.

As U.S. President Jimmy Carter told him, "We don't even let civilians *see* that plane!" Civilians are people who are not in the military.

But as usual, Father Hesburgh made a very good case for what he wanted to do. Somehow, he talked government officials into giving him a ride, but only if he could pass tests they give to astronauts to make sure they can take the stress of high-speed flight. Father Hesburgh even had to learn how to eject from a plane flying at 80,000 feet. That's more than 15 miles above Earth.

He passed! During his flight, he felt the skin pulling back on his face as the plane got close to Mach 1, the speed of sound. At 62, Father Hesburgh was as thrilled as that 10-year-old looking down from the propeller plane piloted by the barnstormer.

"That was a roller-coaster ride I will never forget," he said later.

Throughout his life, Father Hesburgh made many missions for the Vatican, which is the headquarters of the Catholic Church. And after he retired as president of Notre Dame, he continued to make a mark on the larger world. He helped lead several organizations devoted to education, human rights, and world peace. He also helped to develop college sports in positive ways.

He was co-chairman of the Knight Commission on Intercollegiate Athletics. That group was founded in 1989. It was formed to deal with many scandals that had given college sports a bad name. The commissioners believed that college sports would be more honorable and fair if athletes were also expected to do well in the classroom. Today, the Knight Commission still works to promote that policy.

In 2017, the U.S. Postal Service honored the memory of Father Theodore Hesburgh. It made a stamp to recognize him and his life's work. Such stamps, called "commemorative," are made only for very special people who are chosen, as the postal system says, because they "had significant impact on American history, culture, or environment."

HARD TIMES FORGED A LEGEND

Johnny Lujack

In 1935, times were hard in America. It was called the Great Depression, and a lot of people struggled to find work and to support their families. The small town of Connellsville, Pennsylvania, was not far from the coal mining part of the state, and most of its workers struggled, too.

The Lujack family was no different. There were four boys and two girls, and their father, John Lujack, supported them by working as a boilermaker for the rail-

UNIVERSITY OF NOTRE DAME

In the 1940s, Johnny Lujack played both quarterback and running back for the Fighting Irish, as well as playing on defense. He also played for Notre Dame's baseball, basketball, and track teams, and was the first person to letter in four different sports in the first year he was eligible.

road. The Lujacks had little money, but they still had fun. Once in a while, there was money for ice cream from Finley's drugstore. And sometimes, the kids sneaked into the Orpheum Theatre to see movies with cowboy stars, who were like today's superheroes.

One day, 10-year-old Johnny Lujack saw another boy's bike. He didn't have a bike, so he borrowed this one to take a ride. Some people might say he stole it.

Either way, it was a stupid thing to do. But Johnny wasn't a stupid boy, and he wasn't really a bad boy. He knew he made a mistake, and he told his dad, who was playing cards at the time. In 2018, more than 80 years later, Johnny still remembered what his dad told him: "Remind me to give you a beating later."

John Lujack wasn't kidding. In those days, it wasn't unusual if parents spanked their children as punishment. When the card game finished, Johnny did as he was told — he reminded his dad that he was to be punished. They went home, and his dad took a leather strap to his rear end.

Some people would see two lessons in this story. One, never take something that doesn't belong to you. Two, never remind your parents that you misbehaved!

Johnny was fifth child in the Lujack family. They were an active bunch. In 1999, Johnny told a reporter, "In our family, sports was our main recreation because we didn't have any money to do other things."

Johnny also liked to listen to sports on the radio, especially to football games. But not just any football games — *Notre Dame* football games. By 1920, before Johnny was born, the Fighting Irish were famous. Their coach, Knute Rockne, was the most successful coach in major college football. The Irish had players who were legends — George Gipp, known as "The Gipper," and four running backs known as the "Four Horseman." By 1930, the Irish had won four national championships.

Starting in grade school, Johnny's heroes were Notre Dame players. If the Irish won, he was giddy with happiness. If they lost, he felt sick.

The Lujacks had a Philco radio that was big, and sat

on legs. You dialed through its glowing numbers to find the right station. The Lujacks never had enough money to take a vacation, but the old Philco could take Johnny almost anywhere in the world. He had a ticket to a Notre Dame game every Saturday in fall.

Johnny would lie on the floor, between the radio's legs, and listen as the Fighting Irish romped over Army, Ohio State, Kansas, and Southern California. He couldn't wait to read all about it the next day in the Sunday newspaper, The Daily Courier. Wouldn't it be something to play on that team, he thought. But that was just a dream in the head of a boy from nowhere.

Johnny threw himself into all kinds of sports — at school, in sandlots — anywhere kids were playing, Johnny was there. Football, baseball, high-jumping, pole-vaulting, throwing the javelin ... you name it, Johnny was into it.

The Lujacks had a big garden near their house. They grew vegetables like beans and tomatoes that Johnny's mother, Alice, canned and stored for eating during the winter. Every year, the family would get the garden ready for planting in the spring, turning the soil to prepare it for the seeds. On a big farm, workers plow the land with tractors. The Lujack children worked their garden with shovels.

One Saturday, when Johnny was in high school, he had garden duty. It was the same day he was supposed to compete in a track meet. He didn't want to miss it, so he worked fast. But he soon realized that he wasn't going to finish in time. He told his dad, expecting him to say, "Too bad."

But, remember — Johnny was a good boy. His dad knew that. He said, "Why didn't you tell me? Go!"

At Connellsville High School, Johnny lettered in three sports — basketball, track, and football — but his best sport was football. He played on both offense and defense, but he was best at quarterback for the Connellsville Cokers. He was a star, and everybody could see he was special, including somebody he barely knew.

Henry Opperman ran a garage in town. He knew that Johnny was a good football player, and, like Johnny, he loved Notre Dame. One day, when Johnny was 17, Mr. Opperman told Johnny's dad that he knew someone with a connection to Notre Dame who might be able to help Johnny get into the university.

Of course, Johnny was excited, but he thought going to Notre Dame was impossible. How in the world could his family afford to send him? Mr. Opperman said maybe Johnny could get a scholarship. For that, you had to be a good student as well as a good athlete. And Johnny was. In fact, he was the valedictorian of his class. That means he had the highest grades of all the seniors. He was also president of his class.

Mr. Opperman and the man with the Notre Dame connections took Johnny to the campus in South Bend, to introduce university officials to their idea of a great student and athlete. Johnny had never been so far from home — it was 400 miles away.

It was the early 1940s, and America was involved in World War II. A lot of young men were joining the military, and being sent to fight in Europe, against Germany, and to the Pacific, against Japan. Then, as now, America's major service academies — West Point for the Army and Annapolis for the Navy — were very choosy about who was allowed to attend, and it was an honor to be a student at either.

A lot of people in Connellsville wanted Johnny to go to West Point, to play football for Army, and be educated as an officer. Although Johnny met the high bar for admission, his heart was set on Notre Dame.

He wasn't disappointed. When they arrived at Notre Dame, he thought it was the most beautiful place he had ever seen. The place where his Saturday dreams came from. Heaven.

In 1942, Frank Leahy was Notre Dame's football coach. He was the kind of man who would make you work hard by sometimes having fun with you. Johnny recently told a reporter that if a player made a mistake, Coach Leahy might say, "Ah lad, you're not going to get into heaven doing things that way."

Johnny came to like Coach Leahy. That day, Johnny ran, threw some passes, caught some, punted … he spent the afternoon showing off his best moves.

Coach was impressed. He also knew about Johnny's background, and his good work in school. He offered Johnny a scholarship.

Johnny felt like he just won the World Championship

of Everything! He was going to go to Notre Dame! He would get an excellent education *and* he would play for the team that had lived only in his dreams. Yes, he earned it, but he also knew how lucky he was. So many talented people only a little older than he was were going off to war. He was going to school, and to play football.

Johnny enrolled at Notre Dame in the fall of 1942. He became friends with his classmates, and called them the "cream of the crop." In 2018, when he was 93 years old, he told a reporter that what he loved most about Notre Dame was that it "was a place where good things happen to you."

In his first year, Johnny got used to college life, but not varsity football. At that time, freshmen were not allowed to play with varsity teams — that changed in 1968 for most sports, but not until 1972 for football and basketball. But, as in high school, Johnny was interested in other sports, and he joined the basketball, baseball, and track teams.

Sometimes, he played two sports at the same time. Several years ago, Johnny recalled that crazy time for a reporter. "In my first baseball game," he said, "I had two singles and a triple in four at-bats. Between innings, I ran over to the track to do the high jump and javelin. All I did was take my sliding pads off. But it was kind of tough to do the high jump because we had those baggy baseball trousers."

It wasn't unusual for a college guy back then to play more than one sport, but it was unusual to do it on the same day. His teammates would joke, "Hey, Johnny, there's also a swim meet today — maybe you could fit that in."

Johnny was a sophomore, in his second year, when he got a big break. And a hard lesson.

The football team traveled to play the University of Pittsburgh. Although Johnny was now on the varsity squad, he was the second-string quarterback, playing behind a popular senior named Angelo Bertelli. Because they were playing so close to where Johnny grew up, Coach Leahy knew that people who knew Johnny from home would come to see the game. So he let Johnny play quarterback.

In his three years as team leader, Angelo and the team had lost only three games. Now, in 1943, as a senior, he told Coach it was OK to let Johnny play … if you don't care if you lose.

For a while, it looked like they might.

Johnny called a play for the halfback — a running back who takes the ball from the quarterback to carry through or around the defensive line. The halfback was Creighton Miller, who was supposed to run by Johnny's left side to be handed the ball from Johnny. But when the ball was hiked, Johnny turned to the *right* for the hand-off. Oops.

Back in the huddle, Johnny remembered, Creighton wasn't happy. "See my jersey?" he asked Johnny. "It says 'Notre Dame.' That means we're on the same team. Let's try it again."

They tried the same play again. The ball was hiked,

Creighton ran to Johnny's left, and Johnny turned right. Again!

In the huddle, Creighton asked, "Um, Mr. Lujack, was it something I said that upset you?" The team laughed.

They tried the play once more, and this time Creighton got the ball from Johnny. He ran for a touchdown. The Fighting Irish won, 41-0.

After that game, Johnny got another break. But his good fortune was the result of someone else's bad luck. Although Notre Dame students continued to study and play sports, some of them also interrupted their studies to fight in the war. Angelo Bertelli was one of them — in October 1943, he was called by the Marines to go fight in the Pacific. He had played in only six games that season, and now it was Johnny's job to run the team.

That year, Angelo had played well enough in the beginning of the season to win the Heisman Trophy, college football's top award. And Johnny had kept Notre Dame at the top of its game — the Irish won the national championship that year.

After that season, Johnny also was called into military service. For the next two years, he was an officer in the Navy, fighting in Europe. Like Angelo, Johnny was always in danger ... but on the other side of the world. He was hunting German submarines in the English Channel.

When the war was over, both men returned home, safely.

Johnny returned to Notre Dame in 1946, and went right back to school and to the football field. A lot of people say he led the Irish to the greatest years in the university's football history. He played both as quarterback, and on defense, as what we call a defensive back.

That year, the Irish were part of one of college football's most famous games. Army was ranked Number 1, and Notre Dame was Number 2. Army had two outstanding running backs — Doc Blanchard and Glenn Davis. They could run through and around the defensive line. So newspapers called them Mr. Inside and Mr. Outside.

It was shocking that, near the end of the game, neither team had scored. Johnny was playing on defense when Doc Blanchard took the ball and ran down the field all alone, heading for the goal line. It looked like nobody could catch him.

Except the kid from Connellsville.

Remember, Johnny ran track. He was fast. Faster that day, than Doc. He tackled him before Doc could score, and the game ended in a tie, something you never see these days in football, and something that was rare in 1946. Once again, Johnny was the star. And, once again, Notre Dame was the national champion.

In September 1947, Johnny was pictured on the cover of Life, one of the most popular magazines in America. It was Johnny's last year at Notre Dame. He passed for 777 yards, and the team was undefeated. Johnny was elected Associated Press Male Athlete of the Year, he won the Heisman Trophy, and the Fighting Irish repeated as national champions.

Johnny's family was proud of his success. But because of his father's work schedule, his parents never saw him play football or basketball in high school. And because they had little money, they had seen him play only one game at Notre Dame in all four years. For that game, they drove eight hours from Connellsville to South Bend, and drove back home right after the game.

Johnny graduated from Notre Dame in 1948 with a degree in political science. He had played four sports for the Fighting Irish, and had earned varsity monograms — letters — in all four. He was only the third Notre Dame athlete to letter in four different sports. He was the first to do it in his first year of eligibility.

That year, Johnny went to play with the Chicago Bears of the National Football League. In those days, even the pros sometimes played on both offense and defense, and Johnny did too.

The kid from nowhere was now known by everybody in the country. He was a media darling, and in the summer of 1949, he even starred in a radio show, "The Adventures of Johnny Lujack." They were stories about his football days at Notre Dame. Just as Johnny was glued to the radio when he was kid in love with the Fighting Irish, his radio adventures were also enjoyed by kids all over the country.

Johnny played with the Bears for four years. As a

quarterback, he passed for almost 6,300 yards, and his record was 13-5. Twice he was named an All-Pro.

He could have played much longer, but one day, he got a call from his old Irish coach, Frank Leahy. Coach asked Johnny to work with him as an assistant coach at the university. Johnny loved Leahy. He loved Notre Dame. It was a no-brainer — he said yes.

It was the right decision, but after two years, Coach Leahy had to quit for health reasons. Everybody in America expected Johnny to be named the next head coach.

But Notre Dame had a new president, Father Theodore Hesburgh, and his main goal for the university was to improve its academic standing. Father Hesburgh was a man who expected everybody to excel, and he believed that becoming such a successful football power had come at the cost of making Notre Dame an excellent place to learn.

So, instead of Johnny, Father Hesburgh chose a well-respected, 25-year-old high school coach to replace Coach Leahy. He wanted to change the win-at-all-cost attitude.

If you think Johnny was disappointed, you are wrong. Johnny didn't want to disappoint Coach Leahy, but, as he told a reporter in 2018, he never wanted the job of head coach. In fact, he got on his knees and prayed that it wouldn't be offered to him.

He thought he was too young for the job. He joked that if a great coach was a score of 100, *he* was a 0.

He and his wife, Pat, were raising a family, and Johnny wanted to be with them.

God bless you, Father Hesburgh.

In 1954, Johnny and Pat moved to Iowa, where he purchased a Chevrolet dealership, and got down to business.

But in 1958, CBS called. The network wanted him to be a TV broadcaster for New York Giant NFL games. For five years, he worked with another announcer, Chris Schenkel. It was fun, talking about his favorite game for millions of viewers. But in 1962, the Ford Motor Company began advertising during Giants games. When the company learned that Johnny owned a Chevrolet dealership, they fired him.

Today, at 93, Johnny and Pat Lujack split their time between Iowa and the California desert. He has lived the kind of life he used to dream about, from starring in high school to starring at Notre Dame and in the NFL; from serving his country during war, to becoming a TV personality. Johnny's journey is an American story of an American kid from a poor town no one ever heard of. Until they did.

FIRST, YOU SURVIVE

Haley Scott DeMaria

Haley Scott couldn't move. It was dark, and freezing cold. She was lying in a snowbank, staring up at the school bus right next to her. It was upside down.

No one wants to have a nightmare, but Haley was hoping this was one. It wasn't. The incident on the highway was real, not a bad dream. There had been a horrible accident, and Haley was hurt. She might never walk again.

Haley Scott was 18 years old.

HALEY SCOTT DEMARIA

Haley grew up in Phoenix, Arizona, in a sports-loving family. Her uncle played basketball in the NBA. Her aunt swam in the 1976 Olympics in Montreal, Quebec. Her cousin, Coco Vandeweghe, is a top-ranked professional tennis player who, in 2017, made it to the semifinals of two Grand Slam events, the biggest tournaments in the sport.

Everybody in Haley's family was expected to win. They were so competitive that sometimes, after family card games, they didn't talk to each other for days.

When she was little, Haley wanted to be like them, she wanted to be good at sports. She tried a lot of sports, but she felt clumsy. And in the 1980s, most of the girls her age thought playing sports wasn't cool. That it was for boys.

Haley's natural competitive spirit also found a way into the classroom. Her favorite subjects were always history and math. She liked math because it is a very exact study, and perfection made her comfortable. People like this are called "perfectionists."

Haley listened to the radio a lot and to musical plays. Sitting cross-legged on the floor of her bedroom, she sang and dreamed. Oh, wouldn't she love to be able to write those plays, wouldn't she love to sing like Billy Joel or Jon Bon Jovi. But how could someone who felt so gawky ever be a dancer? How could someone who was only 10 years old, but was 5 feet 8 inches tall, ever be graceful? After all, the average adult man is only two inches taller.

Haley thought she would never stop growing. But

soon she would realize that being tall was a gift.

Haley had always loved the water. It was the only place she didn't feel clumsy. By the time she was 3, she was swimming in the backyard pool. She even loved the smell of the chlorine, the odor some pools have that smells like bleach. She swam all the time, and some people said she was part fish.

Haley Scott was still a toddler when she learned to swim in the family pool.

She was still in grade school when she started competing, and she won her first swim trophy when she was 8. She didn't know it at the time, but being taller than most people helps you be a better swimmer. That's because longer bodies make smaller waves. Also, taller people usually have larger muscles, and bigger hands and feet, which generate more power moving through the water.

If Haley felt uneasy about being so much taller than other kids her age, she felt at home in the water. Nobody knows how tall you are when you're swimming. As she got older, she got faster. Haley had found the sport she was good at. When she was wet, she felt strong.

By the time she was in middle school, she was training with the Joe Phillips Swim Club. (Later, Phillips would be her coach in high school.) The club traveled around the state to compete with other swim teams. When Haley was 11, she won her first state championship in the 50-meter freestyle event.

In high school, Joe Phillips taught his swimmers more than proper stroke form, more than how to breathe, and how to build strength. He taught them that when you love what you do, what you're good at, you work hard even when you don't feel like it. Haley learned that just making the effort, sometimes, was the reward.

Almost every athlete who works and races hard gets hurt at some point. Haley was no different. When she was 15, she had a shoulder injury that forced her to stop swimming for six months. It seemed like six years.

After she was healed, Haley jumped back into the water more determined to swim fast than ever before. At the end of her high school swimming career, Haley had won Arizona State swimming championships in the 100 butterfly, 50 freestyle, and team relay events.

She was also a champ in the classroom, graduating with a grade point average of 3.6. In high school, excellent students who are also excellent athletes qualify to be elected as Academic All-Americans by the National

High School Coaches Association. Haley, of course, won that "race," too.

Although sports competition was important to her parents, they urged Haley to choose a college based on the high-quality education it offered, above all else.

Universities with superior sports and academic programs are always looking for students who excel at both. Often, the schools recruit those students. That means they invite them to attend their school. Haley was Notre Dame's kind of student. It recruited her for the next freshman class, so Haley visited the campus.

SCOTT FAMILY

Haley won her first swimming trophy when she was 8.

South Bend, Indiana, couldn't have been more different from Arizona. Arizona was a dry, hot desert. Indiana was humid, green, and freezing in the winter. But as cold as the weather was, the students, teachers, and sports staff were warmly welcoming.

As she walked across the campus, everybody, it seemed, smiled at her. A lot of people asked where she was from, and asked if she needed anything. Notre Dame had a fine academic program, and its swim team was getting better and better. But it was the people at Notre Dame who convinced Haley that she would be at home there.

In the autumn of 1991, Haley joined the Fighting Irish of Notre Dame. She still loved math, and chose it as her major. She was swimming well for the team, and very happy to be a part of the Notre Dame family.

Northwestern University is near Chicago, about 100 miles from South Bend. In January 1992, the Fighting Irish traveled to Northwestern for a swim meet against the Wildcats. During the bus ride back to South Bend through the cold winter night, the weather got mean. Snow blew hard at the side of the bus. The road got slick.

They were only 2 miles from home when the back end of the bus started sliding sideways. The driver tried to control it, but the front end also skidded. Suddenly, the bus plunged over the side of the highway, rolled over, and smashed upside down in the snow.

Inside, the girls were tossed around like rag dolls, against the sides, the roof, and the seats of the bus. When the bus came to rest, Haley crawled out of a broken window and into the snow. But then, she couldn't move.

Nobody was yelling, Tim Welsh, the swimming coach, later told Haley. Anybody who could move was trying to

SCOTT FAMILY

Haley Scott competes in a butterfly event for Notre Dame.

help somebody else as the snowstorm howled. One girl found Haley, and stayed by her side.

It seemed like forever, but finally ambulances came screaming out of the storm. Haley told the medical people and the police that she couldn't feel her legs. Were they were numb from the cold? Or worse?

They took her to the hospital, where the doctor's report was not good. Haley was told that her spine had been crushed. She was told that she probably would never swim or walk again, or be able to have children. As if that wasn't bad enough, there was more sadness and pain to come — the next day, Haley found out day that two of her teammates had died in the crash.

For Haley to have any chance of recovery, the doctors had to operate on her spine right away. They wouldn't know for two days if the surgery was successful. That's how long it took to find out if Haley could move her legs.

Forty-eight long hours went by. Nothing happened.

The doctors prepared her for what the rest of her life probably would be like — a year in the hospital, then a wheelchair, then, maybe, walking with leg braces.

The news seemed to get worse every day. The only thing that helped was that her parents were with her. They told her that the whole Notre Dame campus was praying for her.

Very few people feel strong when they're lying in a hospital bed, unable to move. Haley wasn't like most people. The same mental toughness that had helped her train to be a fast swimmer, and to recover from early injuries, now helped her find an inner strength. She would not be beaten by the bus accident. She would not stop setting goals to make her body better. She would not stop believing that she had a future.

Her resolve — the promise she made to herself to keep trying — wasn't only about moving her body. Her fight was also for the friends she had lost in the accident. She was alive, and they weren't. She owed them her best effort. She vowed that not only would she walk again, she would swim again. That resolve was her tribute to them.

A week later, her mom and dad were in the hospital

room with her when something happened. Haley's big toe moved. It was the first time since the accident that she could feel anything in that part of her body. She screamed with happiness, she broke into laughter and tears. Her parents hugged her, and cried. The medical staff ran into her room, all shouting with joy.

The president of Notre Dame, Father Edward "Monk" Malloy, came to visit. He wanted to pray with her. Haley told him she wasn't Catholic. He nodded, and said, "That doesn't matter. You are Notre Dame."

In that moment, every good thing Haley had believed about Notre Dame became real. She had been at the university only a few months, but everybody there was pulling for her. Every day students lined the hall outside her hospital room to visit and pray. They prayed for her at the Grotto, which is a special, spiritual part of the campus formed by rocks in the side of a small hill. Students she didn't even know put up banners on campus that read "God Bless Our Swimmers." Students, teachers, and staff sent her a huge card that 10,000 people had signed, wishing her well.

One night, Haley was in her wheelchair when her mom rolled her to the window at the end of the hospital corridor. She could see buildings in downtown South Bend. She could see the Pizza Hut, and Notre Dame's Golden Dome, blazing in the night sky. It seemed to shine just for her, and tears ran down her face.

After a few days, Haley could move more parts of her body. More toes. Both legs. After six days she was able to stand, then she could use a walker to move on her own. Next, she was strong enough to use a cane. The surgeon had put two steel rods in her back to hold her spine in place, so she walked slowly, but she was getting stronger.

As a member of the Notre Dame Women's Swimming & Diving Team, Haley had performed so well before the bus accident that in April, she earned a monogram. Getting a Notre Dame monogram is like "lettering" at other schools. It means the athlete has the right and the honor to wear the ND initials on her school jacket.

By then, she was back home in Arizona, recovering. By summer, she was able to slip into the family pool. It felt so good. The cool water welcomed her. This is where I belong, she said to herself.

Haley's battle, however, was far from over. Her legs throbbed, and made it hard to sleep. One night, she woke up and her night shirt was soaking wet. It was blood. The steel rods in her back had broken away from the bone.

She had an operation to repair the damage. It was painful, and it did not go well. Her spine bent forward, and she had to undergo more surgery. Was it ever going to stop?

But this time, the doctors were smiling when she woke up. The operation had gone well. They told her she would walk tall. They told her she would be able to swim.

Haley felt as if her prison door had opened, and she was free. She couldn't wait to get back to Notre Dame.

When she returned, in the fall of 1993, about 20

months after the accident, people treated her like a hero. She restarted her classes, and studied extra hard. But the question loomed: Could she compete?

Coach Welsh was willing to let her try. Haley was back training in the pool, back to the gym to work out. She wanted to swim in a meet only 21 months after a lot of people thought she would never walk again. She and the water were friends again, and Haley felt strong. She didn't need to *win* the meet, she just needed to compete hard.

The meet was at Notre Dame. Her parents traveled from Arizona just to watch her race. The stands were packed with fans screaming for Haley, who would be swimming the 50-yard freestyle event. She would have to swim well in her heat — a preliminary race — to advance to the final. As Haley stepped up to the starting block, all she wanted was to swim well.

At the sound of the horn, Haley flew off the block, dived into the water, and kicked forward. She was gliding, her strokes smooth and strong. The racers approached the end of the race, and the crowd was cheering. When they hit the wall, the loudspeaker blared: "First place, lane three."

The crowd screamed. The noise was deafening. Haley's lane was Number 3. She won the heat, and qualified for the final!

That heat was the last race Haley would ever win. She swam two more years for Notre Dame, but as she told a reporter later, "I never won another race again in college.

And that was really hard for me. But … I learned that I had 'won' something greater. Sometimes when you don't win, you just need a different perspective."

After five operations, after 21 months of recovery, Haley was back. And she had brought a whole university with her. Haley was the bold soldier in a very determined army.

Haley swam in about a dozen more meets while she was at Notre Dame. She wasn't happy about not winning, because the will to train, to race, and to win was still strong. But she learned to accept it. Even though she regained her athletic ability, she wasn't at the high level she once had achieved. She learned that it was more than enough to have survived a terrible accident and to have the full use of her body, even if it wasn't as fast as it used to be.

Haley concentrated on her studies. She had missed too many math classes to catch up, so she changed her major to history. It was hard. She loved it.

In 1995, Haley graduated from Notre Dame. Today, she's married to Jamie DeMaria, whom she met at Notre Dame. They have two kids. In 2008, she and a co-writer wrote a book about that terrible night on an icy highway, and what she learned from the long recovery. The first part of the title, "What Though the Odds: Haley Scott's Journey of Faith and Triumph," is taken from words in the Notre Dame fight song.

A few years ago, she told a reporter for a Notre Dame

magazine how hard it was to write about the worst thing that ever happened to her. But it turned out to be a way to help her continue to heal. She said, "It is so clear that the experience of the bus crash and being at Notre Dame during that time has defined everything and every way I live my life. One of the things that I learned is that you don't go through this alone."

One day, years later, Haley was at a shopping mall near her home in Annapolis, Maryland. She was wearing her old team shirt. A woman asked her, "Did you go to Notre Dame?"

Haley nodded yes. "Were you on the swim team?" Haley nodded. "Were you on that bus?" Yes.

The woman touched her and said, "I prayed for you."

THE ELEGANT EXPLAINER

Red Smith

When Walter Wellesley Smith was 10 years old, he announced that he didn't like his name. He decided he would be Red. Red Smith. You only had to look at him to see why he chose that name. His hair was the color of a forest fire blazing out of his head. He thought "Red" was a better name than "Brick," which was what the other kids called him.

As a kid, Walter Wellesley Smith also thought he wasn't any good at sports. He turned out to be as wrong

NOTRE DAME MAGAZINE

Red Smith won the Pulitzer Prize, journalism's highest honor, in 1976. His sports columns were about "the little piece of the world as I see it, as it is in my time," he said.

as ketchup on ice cream.

Red Smith was born in 1905. He grew up in Green Bay, Wisconsin, where he learned to read when he was 5 years old. The Smith house was full of books. Books on famous people, books on science, storybooks full of adventure. Red devoured them because they took him to places he had never been.

Red was very close to his sister, Catherine. She shared his love of adventure, and his love of reading. Together, they would even look up words in the dictionary.

His father often told stories around the dinner table. His mother read to him from The Saturday Evening Post, a famous magazine with stories about almost anything you could imagine. Red's favorites were the ones about famous sports figures who did goofy things — baseball players who missed trains that took them to their games; football players who ran really fast, but toward the wrong end of the field.

Like other boys his age, Red was interested in sports scores, but he was more interested in the unexpected things people did while they played the games.

A biography is the story of someone's life. Red's biographer — the person who writes it — was Ira Berkow. He quoted Red as saying, "A sense of humor is a precious possession."

There was a lot of laughter in the Smith house, and as he got older, Red would realize what a gift it was. The Smiths had a lot of fun, but Red's parents expected him to work hard. Red's father owned a grocery store, and it was Red's job to deliver groceries from a wagon pulled by a horse. Even if he had been old enough to drive, Red couldn't. In those days, automobiles were a new invention, and, according to his biography, there were fewer than a dozen of them in all of Green Bay.

Another of his chores was cleaning up the breakfast table. "Crumb the table!" his mother demanded, then released him to run outside for a game of baseball.

Red liked to play, but he dropped the ball so much the other kids wondered if he were allergic to it. He was also shorter than most kids, and when you're a kid you never want to be different.

Red liked football, too, but the closest he ever got to that action was shoveling snow off the field before a game other boys would play.

In addition to being short, Red wore thick glasses. The Berkow book says he described himself as being "distinguished by flaming hair, milk-bottle glasses, and the two left feet of a nonathlete."

But he loved being outside. There were a lot of lakes and streams where he lived, and he spent a lot of time fishing. Nature was always able to deliver some kind of adventure.

He would read an adventure story in bed at night, and the next day he would walk through the woods with a head full of tales: This stream is the Nile River, and it's full of crocodiles! Those trees are Sherwood Forest, and Robin Hood lives here!

Red was good at making up stories, at creating pictures in his mind. The books he read and the stories he heard weren't just entertaining, they made him want to know more. They made him curious. What's around that rock? What's under the water? What's that noise behind me?

Some people don't like to be surprised. But surprises make life more interesting. They make you want to know more about what happened. The more you know, the better the story you can tell.

One day when Red was a teenager, according to his biography, he was ambling along a creek in the woods when he saw a guy fishing. The fellow seemed to know what he was doing — fish were practically jumping into his pail.

The man spotted Red, and asked if he wanted to fish too. Of course he did, but he didn't have his fishing rod. The man, whose name was Vince Engel, broke a willow branch off a tree and showed Red how to carve it into a fishing pole.

They sat together on the riverbank, their lines dangling in the water as they chatted. Vince, it turned out, wasn't that much older than Red. He was a student, studying journalism at the University of Notre Dame. Red knew all about Notre Dame from reading the newspaper sports pages.

Red asked Vince why he was studying journalism. Like Red, Vince was a curious guy. He chose journalism, he told Red, because he wanted to dig into things that were happening in the world around him. He wanted to meet people and listen to what they had to say. Maybe, Vince said, he would get a job at a newspaper and report on events all over that world.

When Red went fishing that day, little did he know that he would catch the rest of his life. A long time later, when he was an adult, according to the biography, Red remembered Vince. "He became a hero of mine. I wanted to do what he did."

For the first time, Red understood what it meant to have a goal, and what you had to do to reach it. Red wanted to go to Notre Dame and study journalism. He buckled down in school, studied hard, and got good grades. His hard work was rewarded when he was accepted at Notre Dame.

But the goal was still out of reach. A Notre Dame education was expensive, and Red's family was not wealthy. So after high school, Red went to work for a hardware store, doing paperwork in the back office. He saved money, and after a year, he headed for South Bend. Now he had two jobs — being a student and waiting tables in a local restaurant. In 1923, Red Smith became a member of Notre Dame's freshman class.

At that time, there were very few radio broadcasts. It was before television, and the internet was an idea even a science fiction reader wouldn't believe. People got their news from newspapers, and in the early 1920s, reporters were writing about a new stadium for the Yankees, and about Calvin Coolidge becoming president. And they were writing about the "Fighting Irish" of Notre Dame.

The Fighting Irish nickname became better known when school's underdog football team beat the powerful Army football team in 1913. They did it by fooling their opponents with unusual plays. It's one game that really deserves the label "legendary."

In those days, football was a running game. But Notre Dame star receiver Knute Rockne and quarterback Gus Dorais had been practicing pass plays. Rockne begged the coach to let them run those plays. He believed the only way they could beat Army was by passing the ball.

He was right. The Fighting Irish thumped Army, and newspapers all around the country wrote about it. A lot of people said the pass was an illegal play, but it wasn't. It simply was a play nobody ever used. That game changed everything about the game of football.

About 10 years later, during Red's time at Notre Dame, sports writers were writing about the four guys who made up the football team's backfield — players who set up behind the ball, mostly running backs. Grantland Rice, a famous sports writer for the New York Herald Tribune, had called them the "Four Horsemen of Notre Dame." That's a reference to the Bible's Four Horsemen of the Apocalypse, and his colorful story was read all over the country.

Red was probably like most people on campus who were thrilled by how good the football team was. How it played with imagination. And how good were the newspaper stories it inspired. The football team seemed to represent the excitement of a growing America.

Sometimes Red would run around the track used by the Fighting Irish track team. Some people would say he's *still* running — he was that slow. One story in his biography is that he was running by Knute Rockne, who by then was coach of both the football and track teams. Red was so slow that Coach Rockne asked him to move out of the way so faster racers could use the track.

But Red liked the coach, a warm and energetic man who built champions, and who also liked to have fun. Notre Dame was still an all-male school during Rockne's time, so once, according to the coach's own story of his life, he played the "damsel in distress" in a campus play.

When asked to name their most influential person on campus, most students voted for Knute Rockne. But Red chose John Michael Cooney.

A professor of journalism, Cooney was another adult in young Red's life who taught him not only the value of books, but the value of laughter. Because Notre Dame was a Catholic university, a lot of professors used prayer in their lessons. Cooney would begin his classes by "praying for sense." Then he called the "Litany of the Saints," which other teachers knew as "roll call." During exams he would announce, "Ten minutes left! Not enough time to write anything good, but enough to cross things out!"

If Red was laughing, he was also listening. As explained in his biography, "Some people are sprinters and some are milers," Cooney told the class, using sports analogies. An analogy explains something by comparing it with something else — in this case, writing a story and running a race.

"The sprinter," Cooney explained, "is capable of the brief, brilliant thing. The miler is good for the long grind. Learn what you are and live with it."

Red had proved that he was no miler — or even a sprinter — on the track. But Cooney helped him understand how different forms of writing demanded different skills. How a sports column, for example, uses different reporting tools from those in a story about a presidential election that takes months of research. In all forms of journalism, Cooney made clear, the writer must tell the truth, and that you get to the truth through careful observation.

Although Red had made the right decision to leave home to attend Notre Dame, when he was a senior, something bad happened that made him deeply sad. His beloved sister Catherine died of tuberculosis. That lung disease took thousands of lives in the 1920s. Because, as reported in the biography, Red was "enjoying himself so much" at school, he felt guilty.

In 1927, Red got his degree, but although he was editor of the school yearbook, in all four years at Notre Dame, he never wrote about sports.

After graduation, he looked for a reporting job. It was harder than he thought — looking for a job was like *having* a job. He wrote to 100 newspapers. Most of them figured he would be as good a writer as he was a runner, because they all said "no." Finally, the Milwaukee Sentinel in Wisconsin gave him a job as a general assignment cub reporter

— that is, a junior writer, a kid … a nobody. To get stories, he chased fire engines, ambulances, police cars … pretty much anything that moved. "I loved it," he recalled in his biography, "and thought it was the most exciting thing in the world."

Red was a fast learner. He learned how to find the right person to answer a question. He learned how to craft a sentence. He learned that the difference between almost the right word and exactly the right word was the difference between a lightning bug and lightning.

After a year, Red had written his arm off, but he had yet to get a byline — when the reporter's name is printed under the headline of the story. He looked for another job where he could write about more subjects, and get credit in print for doing it. The St. Louis Star in Missouri offered him a job writing about one of the city's baseball teams.

Two big things happened to Red in St. Louis: He got his first byline, and he developed the easy-read style his editors liked as much as his readers. Unlike traffic accidents, sports gave him an opportunity to write more casually, more colorfully, and he took it.

"I like to report on the scene around me, on the little piece of the world as I see it, as it is in my time," Red was quoted as saying in a book, "No Cheering in the Press Box," by Jerome Holtzman. "And I like to do it in a way that gives the reader a little pleasure, a little entertainment. I've always had the notion that people go to spectator sports to have fun and then they grab the paper to read about it and have fun again."

In St. Louis, Red also met Catherine Cody. Soon, they would marry, and he and "Kay" would start a family. Not long after the birth of their two children, the Smiths moved to Philadelphia, where Red wrote for the Philadelphia Record. That was during the Great Depression of the 1930s, and the $5 a week raise he got was big money when millions of people in America had no job at all.

While he was at The Record, Margaret Mitchell won the Pulitzer Prize for her Civil War novel, "Gone With the Wind." Pulitzer Prizes are awarded every year in several categories of writing and the arts. They are considered America's highest literary — writing — honor. By now, Red was a well-known sports writer, and although fiction was different from journalism, he wanted to write a novel.

He did, and sent it to publishers, but nobody else knows what it was called or what it was even about, because every publisher turned him down. He might be a good writer, but, as Red learned, he was better at writing things he could observe than things he saw only in his own mind. His failure at fiction reminded Red of Prof. Cooney's advice — figure out your strengths, and stick to them.

In 1939, World War II began, and the U.S. became part of it in 1941 after the Japanese bombed Pearl Harbor in Hawaii. The whole country felt unsafe. It was a difficult time, but people pulled together. Sometimes, they had less than what they needed because items, like sugar, gasoline, and nylon, were rationed to use for the war effort. Rationing means that because the supply of some products is limited, they are available only in smaller, controlled amounts.

President Franklin D. Roosevelt believed that sports could boost the nation's mood in this time of war. Red's bosses at the Philadelphia Record sent his columns overseas, where U.S. servicemen and women fighting and supporting the troops in Europe would read them. Red's columns were also syndicated around the U.S. — that is, newspapers in addition to The Record also published them.

In 1945, Red got the call he had been waiting for all his professional life. The New York Herald Tribune, one of the most widely read newspapers in America, wanted him. And he wanted it. The Smith family packed up to move to New York City, where Red became the paper's lead sports columnist.

After the war, America was changing as fast as it did in the first part of the century. Red was at the Herald Tribune barely a year when, in 1947, one of the biggest sports stories of the century broke. Jackie Robinson, a magnificent athlete, became the first black player in major league baseball.

Then, as now, racism was a problem in America. But it was more open and widespread then. People of color often were denied justice in jobs, schools, public transportation. It's called "discrimination" on the basis of color, and it was more the rule than the exception. When he joined the Brooklyn Dodgers, Jackie Robinson received death threats and letters threatening his wife. Some threatened to kidnap his son. People spit on Robinson, they booed him, and it wasn't only baseball fans — sometimes it was the players, too. Wherever Robinson played, everybody in the ball park took sides.

Red took sides, too.

He wrote: "Intolerance is an ugly word, unsightly in any company and particularly so on the sports page where, happily, it does not often appear. … [I]t is fair to say that on most playing fields, a man is gauged by what he can do, and neither race nor creed nor color nor previous condition of servitude is a consideration. Which is one reason why American sports are as eloquent an expression as we have of the spirit of America."

In 1966, the Herald Tribune went out of business. Like a lot of people, Red was heartbroken. He also was without a job.

But not for long. Soon, he was writing his columns in The New York Times. It was a stuffier paper than the Trib, so for Red, it was sort of like going from the playground to math class. But The Times didn't try to change Red; they wanted him to do exactly what he had been doing — entertaining millions and writing as if he had a love affair with the English language.

In 1976, Red won the Pulitzer Prize for distinguished commentary. He was only the second sports writer ever to win a Pulitzer. (In Chapter 7 of this book, you'll find the story of George Dohrmann, a later Notre Dame graduate who also would win a Pulitzer Prize as a sports writer.)

Also in 1976, Red was inducted into the Baseball Hall of Fame for writing about the sport as well as other Hall of Famers played it. In 1981, the Associated Press Sports Editors established the Red Smith Award. Every year since, a trophy with his name on it is given to the writer the organization believes made the best contributions to sports journalism.

A legacy is what people leave for the people who come after them. Red Smith died in 1982, and his legacy is the gift of elegant writing. He was special not only because he understood sports and the people who play and watch them, but also because he understood that sports are part of a larger world.

Shortly before he died, he said in an interview, "Any sports writer who thinks the world is no bigger than the outfield fence is not only a bad citizen, but also a bad sports writer."

HARD LESSONS ON THE HARDWOOD

Muffet McGraw

The nickname doesn't fit the job.

The image of coaches is often tough. Bossy. Impatient and demanding. If you are going to take a high-level college team to all the way to the top of its game, people don't expect you to have a name like "Muffet." Someone named Muffet, people might think, would be happy just to play a game, never mind win it.

But on April 1, 2018, Coach Muffet McGraw took the Notre Dame women's basketball team as high as it could go

. . . all the way to the NCAA championship. With last-second drama, the woman with the fairy-tale name directed a team that was battered by injuries all season way past its problems. A long, outside shot in the last second won the national title for the Fighting Irish. No one saw it coming, but anyone who knows Muffet McGraw wasn't really surprised, either.

Lots of people get nicknames. Sometimes, they're just shorter versions of their given name — "Rob," for example, is often short for "Robert." Sometimes, nicknames come from how people look — like "Rusty," for somebody who has orange hair. And sometimes, nicknames are given to people because of the way they behave, or think.

If you knew a girl named "Muffet," you probably would think of the nursery rhyme, about a girl with that name who was scared by a spider. You might think she got that name because she was meek, and afraid.

Muffet McGraw is afraid of very little. She goes to a lot of basketball games, and when she is on the court, other people are afraid of *her*.

That's because she knows basketball like mice know cheese. If you're not on Muffet's team, you wish you were. When she was a kid and a young woman, Muffet played a lot of basketball. Today, she's a teacher, and her classroom is a hardwood floor, 94 feet by 50 feet, with a basket at each end. Her classroom is on the campus of Notre Dame.

Muffet McGraw teaches the inbound pass, the 2-3 zone defense, she teaches how to get the best position for a rebound. She also shows her team that "winners" strive to do their best even when they're not playing basketball.

What she never tells is how she got her nickname.

Muffet was born Ann O'Brien, the fifth child in a family of eight children in Pottsville, Pennsylvania. It was an active family that seemed to make a competition out of everything. When she was 9 years old, according to "Courting Success," a book about her life, the family vegetable garden was overgrown with weeds. To most kids, pulling weeds was about as much fun as taking a spelling test. Not to the O'Brien girls. Always ready for a contest, they attacked the weeds as if they were invaders from Mars. Who could fill the most bags with the most weeds? Who would *win?*

"I've always been competitive in everything," Muffet said in "Courting Success," "from checkers to who can get the dishes done the fastest."

In the 1960s and '70s, when Muffet was growing up, there weren't as many organized sports for girls as there are today. So Muffet played her favorite sport, basketball, when she could, with whoever was playing it. She was never afraid to push her way into basketball games the neighborhood boys were playing, where she was the only girl. Because she was fast, and because she could dribble (bounce) and pass the ball as well as any of them, the boys let her play. And she was tough — Muffet took as many bumps and elbows to her face as they did. It was part of the game, she knew, and it made her a better player.

She liked playing basketball with the boys, but she also

UNIVERSITY OF NOTRE DAME

Head Coach Muffet McGraw took the Notre Dame women's basketball team to the NCAA championship on April 1, 2018. It was exactly 17 years after she led the Fighting Irish to their first title, in 2001.

hung out with her sisters. By the time she was 11, Muffet was spending a lot of time with an older girl named Nancy. That girl was smart. She was a detective. Maybe you have spent time with her, too — Nancy Drew is the main character is a series of mystery books. Muffet loved reading "The Ghost of Blackwood Hall," and "The Clue in the Crumbling Wall."

She learned a lot from Nancy about being curious, and helping people in need. Nancy wasn't real, but someone who was real showed Muffet the same things — her mother. Anne O'Brien had eight children to look after, but she always had time to make sure everyone around her was all right. Did an ill neighbor need groceries? Did an elderly couple need a ride? Did the local church need volunteers for the cleaning crew?

The O'Briens were not wealthy, but they were rich in compassion — the ability to feel what other people are feeling. Muffet's dad, Joseph, worked in the insurance business, and he volunteered for many years at Chester County Hospital.

At Bishop Shanahan High School, Muffet played point guard on the girls' basketball team. The position was right for her size — she grew to be only 5 feet 6 inches — and it also was right for her personality. Usually, point guards are the best passers and dribblers on the team, and when their team has the ball — that is, they are on offense — they control the attack by calling plays and setting the tempo.

A good point guard needs to be in charge. Even though Muffet wore glasses, and kids sometimes called her "four eyes," she didn't care. On the basketball court, she was in charge.

Muffet liked learning new things. Her favorite school subjects were English and American History. During high school, Muffet had a part-time job as a waitress at the D&K Diner. Like basketball, restaurants can have their own "lingo." A rebound in basketball is called a "board" because it bounces off the backboard. At the diner, Muffet learned, a "GAC with tommy" was short for "a grilled American cheese sandwich with tomato."

In college, she planned to major in sociology, which is the study of people and how they act as individuals and in groups. Her interest in that subject came from her parents — they had always shown concern and compassion toward people, so Muffet did, too. But even though she was a serious student, she also wanted to keep playing basketball. She wanted to go to a college with a women's basketball program, and there weren't a lot of choices. But the first question wasn't where to go, it was could she afford to go to college at all?

In 1973, when Muffet graduated from high school, Saint Joseph's University (SJU) in Philadelphia had a women's basketball team, but it was new, and it didn't offer any aid or scholarships. (At the time, Notre Dame had been admitting females for only two years, and it didn't have a women's basketball team.)

With money she had saved from her restaurant job, and with the help of her parents, Muffet enrolled at SJU. She still had to work part-time to make ends meet, and in keeping with her interest in sociology, she got a job with the county juvenile probation office. It served troubled kids — kids with no parents, no money, and, often, no hope. The job made Muffet realize how lucky she was to have a family like her own. In addition to her office duties, Muffet later ran a basketball program for kids to help keep them off the streets. She volunteered her time to do this.

Muffet was part of the first women's basketball team at

Saint Joseph's. Only in the 1970s did girls start to play organized sports in large numbers. Compared to boys, those numbers were small, but they were growing. Still, many colleges gave far more support to men's teams. Muffet and her SJU teammates, for example, had to buy their own basketball shoes.

Muffet played guard all four years for the SJU Hawks. As a junior and senior, she was captain of the team. In her last year, the team won 23 games, lost only 5, and was rated by one national poll as Number 3 in the nation.

When Muffet graduated, she planned to use her sociology degree to work with others in need, as she had at the probation office. But first, she got married to Matt McGraw, whom she met when he was an assistant coach at SJU.

But, it turned out, basketball — not sociology — would be her career. She didn't know it at the time, but people outside of Saint Joseph's had noticed her ball-playing skill, and how good she was at helping her teammates be better players. They thought she might make a good basketball coach.

When Archbishop John Carroll for Girls, a high school in Philadelphia, offered her a job as its basketball coach, Muffet gladly said yes. It was the perfect way to combine her love for basketball with her desire to teach. In her first year, 1978, the John Carroll Lions went 22-3, and they were undefeated in her second year — 22-0 — when the team won the Catholic League championship. Muffet was named league coach of the year.

Today, the Women's National Basketball Association (WNBA) is more than 20 years old, but in the late 1970s, most people thought paying women to play in a basketball league people would pay to watch was a joke. But some people didn't, and a few of them formed the Women's Professional Basketball League — the WBL. Because Muffet was such a great college player, she was asked by one of the WBL teams to play for it.

It was the California Dreams, who played home games in Los Angeles. Matt and Muffet were both from the East Coast, but moving so far away wasn't a problem. No one ever thought women would be paid to play basketball, and here was Muffet's chance to make history playing the game she loved. So, in 1980, they moved to California.

The founders of the league had hoped the 1980 Summer Olympics in Moscow would shine a light on some of their players, who would be part of the U.S. team. The WBL hoped to use the popularity of the Olympics to boost the league. But when the United States decided not to participate in the Olympics over disagreements with the Soviet Union, the host country, the chance was lost.

During the 1980-81 season, the WBL struggled. One day, the Dreams were on the East Coast to play a game against the New Jersey Gems when the team ran out of money. The players were told there was no money to buy tickets to fly them back to California. Luckily, the parents of one of Muffet's teammates paid for everybody to get home.

So the door to Muffet's playing career slammed shut. Then, another one opened wide.

Her college, Saint Joseph's University, was looking for an assistant coach for the women's team, and Muffet was ready, willing, and able. She and Matt moved back to Pennsylvania. A year later, she took a bigger job, head coach, at nearby Lehigh University, where she stayed for five years.

Between 1982 and 1987, Muffet led the Lehigh Mountain Hawks to success they had never seen — they won more than twice as many games as they lost, 88 to 41. In her first year, Muffet was named East Coast Conference Coach of the Year. In the 1985-86 season, the women's team won the most games in Lehigh's basketball history.

By now, Muffet was a well-known coach of women's basketball. By now, it was almost 15 years since the first female freshmen had been admitted to the University of Notre Dame. Although the 10-year-old women's basketball team had done OK, the university wanted more than "OK" — it wanted "excellent." When the head coach job opened in 1987, Muffet McGraw wondered what it would be like to lead the Fighting Irish into the future.

Like her dad and her brothers, Muffet had been a fan of Notre Dame football since she was a kid. But Muffet did not apply for the basketball coaching job.

Sure, she hoped to advance in her career, but she was 31 years old, and she wasn't sure she was ready for such a high-profile job. After all, Notre Dame was at the top of everyone's list of competitive college sports.

At the time, according to Notre Dame Magazine, she and Matt were golfing one day. Muffet was in the middle of her golf swing when Matt yelled, "You should have applied!"

It was all the support she needed. A week later they went to South Bend, where Muffet applied for the job. The athletic director, Gene Corrigan, was blown away. He later told a Notre Dame staff reporter, "If we searched for an entire year, I don't think we would find anyone better suited for our program."

Soon after taking the job at Notre Dame, Muffet and Matt were invited to dinner with Father Hesburgh. He had just retired as president of the university. He was well-known in the U.S. and around the world for helping people — something a student of sociology would find noble — and in 35 years at Notre Dame, he had made big changes. The university was good at sports when he got there, but now it was also a fine academic institution. During Father Hesburgh's time, Notre Dame had begun to admit not only women, but more students of color.

At dinner that night, Father Hesburgh told stories of going to Mexico to help make voting in that country more fair. He talked about going to the American

South to address how poorly African-Americans were treated. Muffet later said it was one of the most inspiring dinners she ever had.

Muffet was especially impressed by the role Father Hesburgh played in getting the Civil Rights Bill passed in 1964, when she was only 9. That federal law made it illegal to deny anyone his or her rights to what society had to offer all Americans — voting, education, housing … everything that helped people prosper, and be better citizens.

The Civil Rights Bill paved the way for a law known as Title IX that was passed when Muffet was in high school. It gave girls the same chance to play sports as boys. At that time, 1972, there were 3.9 million student-athletes in high school, and 3.6 million of them were boys. The law helped boost girl power.

In "Courting Success," which Muffet co-wrote with Paul Gullifor in 2003, she recalls leaving the dinner with Father Hesburgh feeling even more inspired about her passions — teaching and winning. She was happy to be in a position to teach young women the value of working hard — on the basketball court, in the classroom, in the world beyond. Because hard work makes you a responsible person, and probably a successful one, too.

Muffet taught her players to be on time. If somebody was late for the team bus, it left without her, and the player had to figure out by herself how to catch up with the rest of the team. She taught her players to sit in the front of the classroom. She taught them to dress well, to represent Notre Dame in the best light.

MIKE BENNETT/ UNIVERSITY OF NOTRE DAME

The coach upholds the tradition of cutting down the net after her Fighting Irish basketball team captured the national title on a dramatic, last-second shot. The team had struggled with injuries all season, but still found a way to win.

Success, indeed, was the result. The Fighting Irish went 20-8 in Muffet's first season as head coach. Now, in 2018, it has had only one losing season since. In 2001, Muffet led Notre Dame to the top of the mountain — her team won the National Collegiate Athletic Association National Championship. The team has made the NCAA tournament every year since 1995-96, and eight times it has made the Final Four — a national measure of excellence. And it will be a long time before anyone forgets the drama of the team's struggle all the way to the 2018 national championship.

Muffet McGraw has been voted Associated Press Coach of the Year, and Big East Conference Coach of the year. She is one of only six NCAA coaches in the top division, male or female, with 800 wins, eight Final Fours, and six NCAA title games.

In 2017, she was voted into the Naismith Memorial Basketball Hall of Fame. Named for James Naismith, who invented the game in 1891, the hall honors the best players, coaches, referees, and contributors to the game.

Just as notable as success on the basketball court is the academic success Muffet's teams can claim. Notre Dame is only one of four basketball programs in the U.S. to play for the national championship in the same year it graduated all of its players — and the Fighting Irish have done that five times. And for 10 years in a row, Notre Dame's women ballers had perfect graduation rates.

A lot of the team's success, Muffet wrote in her book, is because Notre Dame looks for a certain kind of student-athlete. "A certain person comes to Notre Dame," she wrote. The university looks for people with integrity and high standards, people with a bigger world view than just sports. "We don't promise [new players] anything except a good education," she wrote.

Many of her former players have gone on to successful careers in the WNBA and other areas. Ruth Riley, who played center on the 2001 National Championship team, later became general manager of the San Antonio Stars, a WNBA team now known as the Las Vegas Aces.

"I learned how to handle pressure, what it takes to be

a leader, and how to balance my faith, family, academics, and basketball," Ruth said in the foreword to Muffet's book. "I will forever be grateful to Coach McGraw for giving me the opportunity to attend Notre Dame, for instructing me, guiding me, and pushing me to achieve my academic and athletic goals, and, most of all, for the continual support she shows in my life outside of Notre Dame."

The McGraw home is just outside of South Bend, Indiana. If you were to go there and ring the doorbell, it would play "Victory March" — the Notre Dame fight song. Many years ago, a man from another college called Muffet and asked her to think about taking a job at his college.

"I told him, no thanks," she wrote in her book. "I already have the best job in the world."

5

THE VOICE IN THE WIND

George Blaha

At night, as winter winds raced each other across the middle of Iowa, 10-year-old George Blaha snuggled under the blankets with his little red radio. He turned off the lights and pressed the radio against his ear. His parents thought he was asleep, but he was in school — sports announcing school. It was the 1950s, and George was learning about sports by hearing the voices on the radio talk about them.

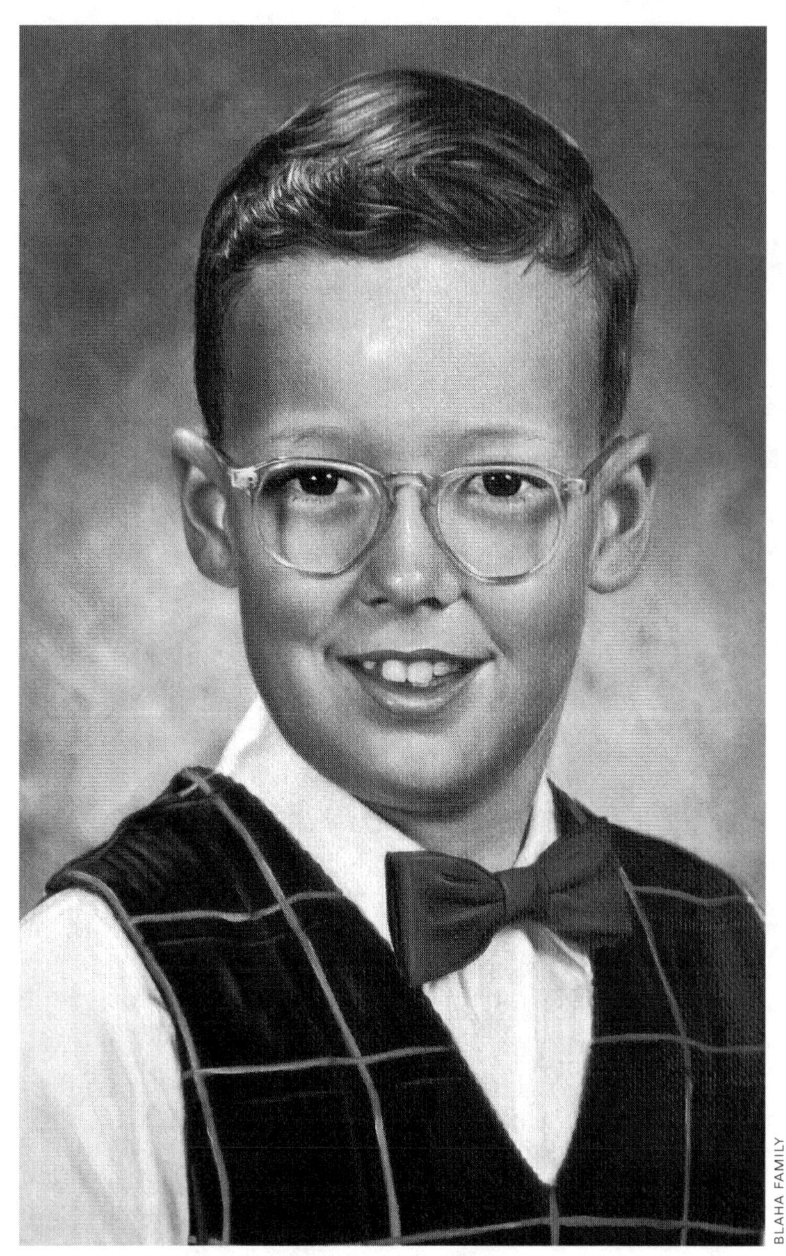
BLAHA FAMILY

As an 8-year-old, George Blaha was both formal and fun.

He learned about basketball and football from Iowa Hawkeyes announcers on WHO in Des Moines, Iowa. He learned about baseball and all sports from voices on WJR in Detroit, Michigan, KMOX in St. Louis, Missouri, and KDKA in Pittsburgh, Pennsylvania. And he listened to his hometown Marshalltown High School Bobcats on KFJB in Marshalltown, Iowa.

"The little red radio had gold along the dial," George remembered as an adult nearly 60 years later. "I would imagine it was a basketball court."

By the time his family moved to Michigan when he was 13, George was listening to a lot of sports on a lot of stations all over the middle part of America. He paid attention not just to the action, but to how different announcers described it. Little did he know that one day, thousands of people would be picking *his* voice out of the air. He would be painting pictures for them with *his* words, and not just on radio, but on TV and streaming over the internet.

Today, in 2018, George Blaha is known as the "Voice of the Detroit Pistons," whose NBA games he has been calling for 40 years. He also announces football games for the Michigan State Spartans on WJR — the same station he'd heard as a kid.

As a boy, George listened to other kinds of radio programs that found their way to his house over the air waves. He liked to listen to music, especially rock 'n' roll, which was new in those days. He played games with himself, trying to find stations from faraway places like KOMA in

Oklahoma City, and WHB in Kansas City, Missouri.

It was fun to collect things that only needed to be plucked out of the wind.

George liked to talk about his interests — sports, and rock 'n' roll music. And George talked a lot. Even as a boy, he had what people call the "gift of gab." George was not shy, and he seemed to have something to say that people liked to hear. George made a lot of friends.

Grayling, the Michigan town where his family moved right before George went to high school, is not very big. It was so small that most of the people in town knew each other. Its residents were hard-working people living in the heart of the American Midwest. The small town was the perfect place for a friendly kid with a lot to say to develop the easy manner that would help him when he was an adult who explained games to people he would never see, or know.

As a youngster, George's best sport probably was baseball. But his eyesight wasn't the best, and once kids got old enough to throw curveballs, he recently recalled, "I was in trouble."

Vernon Blaha, George's father, was a doctor. Education was very important to him. So for high school, George was sent to a Jesuit school, Campion High in Wisconsin, a very good academic boarding school. That means the students live as well as study there. Campion's athletic teams were also strong, so strong that George got cut even from the junior varsity basketball team.

"Campion was a Class A sized sports school," he said,

BLAHA FAMILY

George, 19, in what was known then as the main quad on the campus of Notre Dame.

"and I was a Class C or Class D starter in basketball and football."

Ever since his bedtime stories were told by men describing games in distant cities, ever since George would hide under the covers with the red radio, he had wanted to be a sports announcer. George wasn't good enough to play sports competitively at Campion, so he did the next best thing — he announced them at the school's games. He even taped a few for the campus radio station. It helped him with his announcing skills that Campion had a student radio station, where George broadcast a game now and then, and was a disc jockey on a show called "Blaha Blast." It was the true starting point for his career.

And even though his father, Vernon, was amused by his son's ability to describe games on TV, Vernon thought you wouldn't go as far as you wanted in life without a college degree from a very good school.

The University of Notre Dame had a reputation as a fine academic institution. Its history also was filled with famous sports stories — about the athletes who played games, the coaches who taught them, and the drama of its legendary football teams. It was, like sports itself, a place where some dreams died, but a lot of them also came true. It was a place known for people who never stopped dreaming.

Notre Dame and George seemed like a perfect match. He was a good student, and a good kid who stayed out of trouble. And even if he wasn't a great athlete, he was still crazy about watching and describing sports for others. When Notre Dame accepted him as a student, he knew he had found a home.

In 1962, when he was a freshman, George discovered a lot of his classmates were like him — they were interested in combining sports and the business of sports. Broadcasting was that kind of business, where you were

In 2011, George and Mary Blaha visited with Father Theodore Hesburgh, who was president of Notre Dame when George was a student.

always around sports even if you weren't playing them. As George put it, he was in "high cotton," an expression that means he was right where he wanted to be.

George was most impressed by two people who were at Notre Dame during his days there. One was football Coach Ara Parseghian, even though George knew him only to say, "Hi, Coach." But the coach's ability to motivate and teach a struggling football team seemed to inspire everyone on campus somehow. Coach Parseghian took Notre Dame's team back to the top of the college football world, where the Irish had been in the glory days of Knute Rockne and Frank Leahy — see Chapter 1, about Johnny Lujack, to learn more about them.

The other person who was important to George was Father Hesburgh, the president of the university. George never met Father Hesburgh when he was a student, only later, when he was an adult. But, recently, George remembered Father Hesburgh's vast influence over every part of Notre Dame — his high academic standards, and his concern for human rights, in America and around the world. "We all went to Notre Dame needing direction," he said of other students in his class, "or some kind of boost. Hesburgh gave us that. He gave us a confidence that came with just being there. That has served me all my life."

As seniors, George and his roommate, Bill, both talked about wanting to get jobs in sports after they graduated. Neither was a good enough athlete to be a professional player, but their common goal was to get a job in the business of sports, in the business of making games come alive for fans. So they made a plan to get noticed even before they graduated from Notre Dame.

They went to a local high school basketball game. As they sat in the stands, they recorded themselves calling the action. George was the play-by-play announcer, and Bill did the color commentary. They sent the tape to a man named Frank Crosiar at radio station WJVA in

South Bend. He was the public address announcer at Notre Dame football games.

They also sent the tape to other stations, hoping someone would recognize their talent.

Of all the people who received the tape, only one replied — Frank Crosiar. He advised the young men to forget about a career in broadcasting, that they "would never make it in this business."

Well, Crosiar might have been a fine announcer himself, but he was not a good judge of potential. Eventually, Bill became a prize-winning newspaper sports journalist, and George would realize his dream, too, even if he took a few side trips along the way.

George's degree from Notre Dame was in economics. To please his father, he went to graduate school, and got a master's degree in business administration — an MBA — at the University of Michigan. Then he set out to prove that Crosiar was wrong.

Michigan is shaped like a left-hand mitten, and the town of Adrian sits near the bottom of it. George recently remarked that "Nobody ever drives by Adrian. You have to get off the highway and go find it."

When George found Adrian, he found his future. He was hired at WABJ radio as the sports director and assistant news director. He worked all day at the station, and at night, he was the man behind the microphone, doing the play-by-play for whatever sport was in season for the Adrian High School Maples.

Although he was out of school, George was still learning. He got to know each player — he found out what subjects he liked in school, what his favorite music was, something about his family ... George was learning the "people" skills that made him a better storyteller on the radio. If the announcer knows something about the players in addition to how they play the game, the fans are more interested in what happens to them, and to the rest of the team. When George called a game, it was as if he was on the squad. He was one of them.

With his MBA, George could have gone to a big business in a big city, like Detroit. He could have made a lot of money working with important people who wore suits every day. But that's not what George wanted. He wanted to be the voice the Maples deserved. He wanted to follow his dream, not the money.

George did so well in that small town that he was noticed in bigger cities. He was offered a job by WJIM radio in Lansing, the capital of Michigan, where he first called a Michigan State football game. But he still loved broadcasting high school games, and one of them was the 1974 state Class B basketball championship game.

You wonder what that station manager in South Bend would say now, because the tape of *that* game led to an offer from powerful WJR in Detroit to be the play-by-play announcer for the Pistons. It was George's dream job, it was the league he watched on TV with his dad in their living room in Michigan.

Over the years, George became famous as a sports

broadcaster — his colorful way of describing plays is copied by announcers all over America. He is known for such catchphrases as:

> Lays it up, lays it in!
> Fires, fills it!
> Flips it up, fills it up!
> Scoops it, scores it!
> Measures, and makes!
> Rip-down rebound!
> Nothing but sweet, sweet string music!

You might notice a few things all those descriptions have in common. One is the use of "alliteration." That's when the same letter or sound occurs at the beginning of more than one word in a string of them. People remember these terms because they are kind to the ear. Like music.

Two, many of George's descriptions are short — some people would call this an "economy of language." As he told the Detroit News in 2013, "You can't mess around if you want to describe the game in a timely manner and not fall behind. A lot of [my catchphrases] were born out of necessity. I think [saying] the 'glasser' is quicker than [saying] the 'backboard.'"

This economy — spoken by an announcer who got a Notre Dame degree in economics! — is something George learned by listening to all those games on radio when he was a kid.

In 2018, George could still remember, word for word,

how Harry Caray called Cardinal baseball games in the 1960s. "With everybody else," George recalled, "it was, 'The count is no balls and 2 strikes,' or '0 and 2.' Caray just said, 'Two strikes and nothing on the batter.'

"So when I got to working Pistons games, instead of '3 minutes, 20 seconds left in the quarter,' I'd say: '3 and 20 to go.'"

Basketball, George learned, moves so fast that if you are the announcer and listeners are depending on you to keep up with the action, you have to find words that save half a second here and there. "Most guys," George said, "say, 'Jump shot off the backboard.' I say, 'Leaner off high glass.'"

Even though George travels about 50,000 miles a year to announce all the Pistons' games, even though he's at Michigan State for football, even though he's the go-to guy for recording local Detroit commercials, he still finds time to help others. He knows he didn't get to where he is all by himself.

He raises money for organizations that help young people in the inner city, for young women who have been abused, and for people with developmental disabilities. A lifelong dog lover, George also supports groups that help stray and abandoned dogs in Detroit.

When he does find time to relax, George and his wife, Mary, watch the eagles fly above their Northern Michigan home. If you were to visit, you would hear music coming from his boat on O'Rourke Lake. It would be from the early days of rock 'n' roll.

THE IMPACT PLAYER

Pete Duranko

Pete Duranko had huge hands. That's a good thing for a football player — big hands make it easier to grab people. When you're a defensive tackle, like Pete, your job is to stop the other team's running backs carrying the ball, and throw them down.

How big were Pete's hands? So big you could slip a quarter through his class ring.

One day, Pete wasn't using his hands to grab people.

He was using them to grab the ground. Standing on his hands, he used his arms like legs and his hands like feet to walk upside down from the Notre Dame Stadium goal line to the 10-yard line.

His Fighting Irish teammates looked on, some of them clapping at how Pete could walk so far with his feet held high in the air. But he had just begun. Pete wasn't walking on his hands to amuse the team during a break in football practice, he was trying to win a bet. Some of the guys said there was no way anyone, especially someone his size — 6 feet 2 inches tall and 235 pounds — could walk on his hands the full length of a football field. That's 100 yards!

Before he came to Notre Dame, Pete was a standout player at Catholic High School in Johnstown, Pennsylvania. Pete was born in Johnstown, a small town of about 20,000 people. But Johnstown is a big name in football — a lot of players from the area later became famous, including Joe Montana, Joe Namath, and Johnny Lujack, whose story is told in Chapter 1 of this book.

Pete was the oldest of nine Duranko kids. He was always bigger than his friends, and sometimes he seemed a little scary. But that's only until you got to know him.

In his three years at Johnstown Catholic High School, from 1959 to 1961, Pete played on the offense. He was a fullback who carried the ball when the quarterback handed it off to him. It was only later, at Notre Dame, that his true gift as a defensive player was recognized. As a running back, he was tough to tackle. He seemed to be able to run right over the defense like a truck rolling over a bump in the road, so he got a nickname — "Diesel."

The Conemaugh River winds through Johnstown. In 1889, it broke through a dam and flooded the whole town, killing more than 2,200 people. After the town rebuilt, the banks of the river were popular places for people to gather. One day, Pete and some of his friends were at the river. He saw a little girl fall into the water. She was screaming, and helpless. It looked like she was drowning. Pete grabbed a tree branch and extended it over the water. The girl grabbed it, and he pulled her to shore. Her name was Delcine Herman. She was 5 years old. He was 12 years old. He saved her life.

Pete studied hard in high school. And in addition to playing football, he ran track and competed in the shot put. That's a 12-pound metal ball competitors throw from shoulder height, heaving it with one hand. Whoever throws it the farthest wins.

But football was the sport that put Pete in the spotlight. Today, Johnstown Catholic High School is known as Bishop McCort Catholic High School. When Pete graduated in 1961, he had set the school record for scoring the most touchdowns — 49. That record held for almost 60 years — until 2017. He *still* holds the record for yards gained by rushing (running with the ball) — 3,234. And he is third in total points scored (302), a record he held until 2009.

As the third-leading scorer in Pennsylvania high school

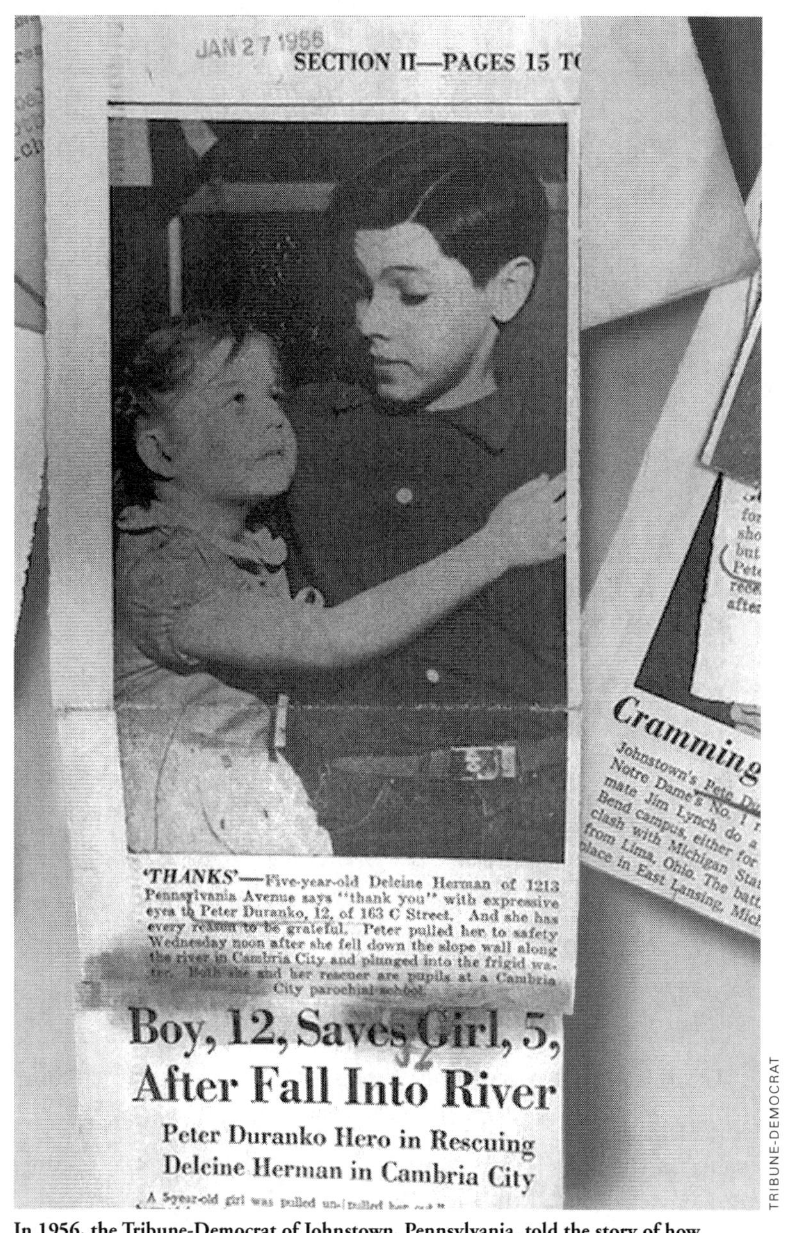
JAN 27 1956

SECTION II—PAGES 15 T

'THANKS'—Five-year-old Delcine Herman of 1213 Pennsylvania Avenue says "thank you" with expressive eyes to Peter Duranko, 12, of 163 C Street. And she has every reason to be grateful. Peter pulled her to safety Wednesday noon after she fell down the slope wall along the river in Cambria City and plunged into the frigid water. Both she and her rescuer are pupils at a Cambria City parochial school.

Boy, 12, Saves Girl, 5, After Fall Into River

Peter Duranko Hero in Rescuing Delcine Herman in Cambria City

TRIBUNE-DEMOCRAT

In 1956, the Tribune-Democrat of Johnstown, Pennsylvania, told the story of how 12-year-old Pete Duranko saved a 5-year-old girl from drowning in a local river.

football, Pete was named by the Associated Press to the all-state team when he was a senior. He was also named an all-star, and years later, was voted into the Pennsylvania Hall of Fame. So football talent was why colleges came calling at the Duranko house. Some of them wanted him so badly that they even sent airline tickets for him to visit their campuses.

One of those universities was Notre Dame. He went to visit the campus in South Bend, where he met another high school player named Jim Smith. That year, 1961, Jim, was the fourth-leading scorer in Pennsylvania. The boys had a lot in common, and they became friends. They talked about Notre Dame, about how both of them had been contacted by the university. Little did they know that day that both would get scholarships from Notre Dame, both would play football for the Fighting Irish in the fall of 1962, and that they would be roommates.

Not long ago, Jim remembered one evening after dinner when he and Pete were walking back to their room. Suddenly, Pete said, "Watch this," and hopped onto his large hands, sticking his feet high in the air. He announced that he was going to walk on his hands all the way back to their room.

Their room was on the fourth floor of the dormitory. A crowd of students gathered to watch, and Pete did not disappoint them. He was a strong athlete, but he was also a showman who loved to entertain. Moving with purpose upside down on his huge arms, he plodded up

COURTESY BISHOP McCORT CATHOLIC HIGH SCHOOL

As Number 11, Pete was a star fullback on the Johnstown Catholic High School team in 1961.

the stairwell, one step at a time. At the fourth floor, other students applauded wildly. Because of such strength, according to one of his teammates, Pete was known as "Superman."

Today, Jim works part time in his family's hotel and restaurant business in Lancaster, Pennsylvania. He remembers Pete had a tremendous work ethic, meaning that once he set a goal, he totally committed to reaching it. Pete not only wanted to do his best at football, Jim said, he wanted to be the best at everything he tried. That included his studies.

When Pete and Jim were at Notre Dame, there was a rule that all dorm lights had to be off by midnight. Pete would turn off the light, then get into bed to study under the covers. "He earned every grade," Jim said. "He was very studious and loved Notre Dame."

He also loved to have fun. Sometimes, Pete the Showman played the harmonica for his classmates. Sometimes he sang — "The Ballad of Black Bart" was about a stagecoach robber in the Old West. "He was fun to be around because *he* was fun," Jim remembered.

In 1963, Pete started his Fighting Irish football career as a fullback, the position he played in high school. The team had not been doing very well for several years, and it still struggled. But in Pete's second year, everyone was excited because Notre Dame had a new coach named Ara Parseghian. Pete was excited not only because Coach Parseghian brought new energy to the team, but because Pete had a new position to play — linebacker. He was moving from the offense, where he was only a backup running back, to the defense, where he was a starter, and his job was to stop the people who were carrying the ball.

Once, Pete told Jim after he graduated, Coach Parseghian was asked what would happen when the team reached its breaking point. "Breaking point?" Coach repeated. "We have no breaking point."

During his pro career, Pete said that the experience with Coach Parseghian "was a blessing for us all."

But the 1964 season wasn't a blessing for Pete. In the opening game of that season, Pete made a big play, intercepting a pass by the opponent, Wisconsin. But later in the game, Pete suffered a wrist injury so bad that he had to sit out the rest of the season.

When he returned for his junior year in 1965, he was

UNIVERSITY OF NOTRE DAME

Pete played offense in high school, but at Notre Dame, he became a standout player on defense. His coach, Ara Parseghian, once said, "If I had 10 more players like Pete Duranko, we'd have won 11 national championships. He was the face of Notre Dame."

healthy, and he had a new position yet again. As a defensive left tackle, Pete finished the season with the second-highest number of tackles on the team — 95. In one game alone, against North Carolina, Pete had 14 tackles, a huge number. The next year, in 1966, he had 73 tackles, and played a key role on a team that was second in the U.S. for scoring by the defense (3.8 points per game). That year, the defense also shut out six of its 10 opponents. That means they held more than half of their opponents scoreless. Over the whole season, Notre Dame's opponents scored only five touchdowns — a remarkably low number.

After three seasons under Coach Parseghian, the Fighting Irish won the national championship. That year, Pete was named a first-team All-American by United Press International and the American Football Coaches Association. After that, he played in the 1967 College All-Star Game in Chicago.

After the championship season, Coach Parseghian said about Pete, "If I had 10 more players like Pete Duranko, we'd have won 11 national championships. He was the face of Notre Dame."

Pete also earned the respect of many of the teams he played against. Long after he stopped playing football, one of Pete's former teammates was talking to a man from another university who had played against Pete. The man remembered that, early in their game, Pete knocked him down so hard he barely knew what hit him. He started to get up, and saw Pete standing over him, smiling. Pete held out his hand to help the opponent up, and said, "It's going to be like this. All. Day. Long."

Pete graduated from Notre Dame in 1967 with a Bachelor of Arts degree. He moved to Denver, Colorado, to play football for the Broncos, an NFL team that also had been struggling for years. He played for eight seasons, and in 1973, Pete helped the Broncos to their first winning season in team history. Now, at 250 pounds, he was part of a defense that was so big and so good at stopping the offense that it was called the "Orange Crush," after the color of Denver's uniforms.

Pete played two positions for Denver, linebacker and defensive end. Both relied on his hard-charging style of play, where really big men crashed into each other all afternoon. If you play those positions, after a game all you want to do is sit in a hot tub. Sometimes, it can be days before your body stops hurting. That's true today, but when Pete played, it was worse. The equipment in those days didn't have the same protection that helmets and pads have today.

Football is a contact sport — part of the game is running into people. You might have contact in basketball, but it's not part of the plan, it's an accident. In football, you hit and get hit on purpose. Even if your muscles and bones stop hurting later, sometimes you get a concussion. That's a kind of brain injury that sometimes doesn't heal. Often, the damage doesn't show up for years.

Pete and his wife, Janet, moved back to their hometown of Johnstown. He was done with football, but he wasn't done with learning. He enrolled at St. Francis University and earned a master's degree in industrial relations. That's a kind of business degree that looks at how bosses and workers relate to each other. Pete took a job as a manager with a steel mill in Johnstown. Just as they did when his job was football, his co-workers at the mill called him a wonderful guy.

In 2000, about 26 years after his last game as a football player, Pete was told he had a disease, ALS. The news was worse than getting hit by an entire offensive line. ALS stands for amyotrophic lateral sclerosis; it's also known as Lou Gehrig's disease. Gehrig was a famous baseball player for the New York Yankees. He died from ALS in 1941, and before he made it famous, a lot of people had never heard of ALS.

The disease makes the brain less and less able to send signals to the rest of the body. So, eventually, every body function — from moving muscles to chewing to breathing — is affected. It gets worse over time, and there is no cure. It's very hard to know why anyone gets ALS, but a lot of experts believe being hit in the head and getting concussions is a big risk. There is a lot of concern that football can lead to all kinds of brain damage, including ALS.

In 2010, as people became more and more aware of the danger of repeatedly being hit in the head, Pete gave an interview to a website called Bleacher Report. "When we were in the game," he remembered, "if you didn't play, you'd go 'highway.' Meaning you got released [cut from the team]. This made you play through all sorts of injuries, especially concussions."

A year after that interview, Pete died from brain disease. He was only 67. When he retired from playing football in 1974, he had no idea that getting hit so much when he was young might be the reason why.

Not long after Pete's terrible diagnosis in 2000, the steel mill closed, and he was out of a job. Worse, nobody would hire him for another job, because he had ALS. And even though Pete had had a long career in the NFL, for years the league ignored him. But, thanks to help of his friends and former Notre Dame teammates Jim Smith and Tom Sullivan, the NFL did assist the Durankos with medical equipment and the cost of care.

Today, many former NFL players have sued the league because they say it knew the risks players were taking, but didn't tell them. Many players have suffered terribly from brain injuries, and all sports now realize the danger of concussions.

But even after his diagnosis, Pete still had some life to live, and he did what he had done his whole life. He put on the smile of a showman, and started giving speeches to elementary school kids about the value of hard work and believing in yourself. He was funny, and kids loved him. Until his strength was taken away, maybe he even walked on his hands.

As the ALS began to take over his body, Pete spent time

with other groups in need of his special gift — elderly people, and those who also had ALS. As told in a story in the Pittsburgh Post-Gazette, Pete said, "It's all about attitude. For me, that comes from football. You don't give up. You do the best you can and keep fighting."

Pete also knew that not everybody had his strong spirit. He helped them, too. He spent time with people who were close to death, and told them, "It's OK to cry and complain and moan. Go ahead. Let it all out. But do it for half an hour a day, then find something you enjoy doing. Make the best of what you have."

Eventually, Pete was in a wheelchair. Still, he kept speaking to groups, including ex-NFL players with ALS. Jim Smith visited Pete, and found that, even though he no longer had a big, strong body, Pete still had a big sense of fun. Jim asked how he managed each day.

Pete smiled, "I play golf. Every day."

"What?"

"Yes, look." Pete took out his laptop, and showed Jim the video golf game he was playing.

In true Notre Dame style, a lot of Pete's classmates recognized his special place in their world. In 2016, to honor Pete, a fund was created by the Class of 1966 — the year he would have graduated, had he not sat out a year. It is called the Pete Duranko Student-Athlete Safety Fund, and the money is used to study head injuries.

An autopsy is a medical exam of a body after death. Doctors perform an autopsy when they want to learn more about why someone died. In Pete's autopsy, his brain showed a disease called CTE — chronic traumatic encephalopathy. It's caused by repeated blows to the head. Boxers often get CTE, as do soldiers who were close to exploding bombs and grenades. Football players, too, sometimes get CTE, which a lot of people believe can cause ALS.

After Pete died, the writer of a Bleacher Report story a year earlier recalled their conversation. "In our talk," he wrote in another story, "he did not lament his fate of having a terminal disease at all. Duranko only spoke of offering help to others. … Thank you [Pete] for giving people like me a reason to have hope for the human race."

Pete Duranko gave hope to a lot of people, including the little girl he saved from drowning. She never forgot him — 55 years later, Delcine Herman Caddy sang at his funeral.

TO TELL THE TRUTH

George Dohrmann

A few hundred people sat in the stands of a school gym watching young boys play basketball. One boy passed to his teammate, who turned the wrong way, and the ball bounced out of bounds.

The coach screamed curses at the kid who missed the pass. The boy's shoulders drooped, and he slunk toward the bench. He knew he had made a mistake, but the coach didn't stop yelling. His face purple with rage, he called the player useless, he said he wasn't worth the cost of his sneakers. He called him an idiot, he called him lazy, stupid, and weak. He wondered out loud why he should waste any more time on him.

George Dohrmann, one of the spectators in the stands, was shocked. This was a game. These were kids who should be having fun. Sure, everyone wanted to play well, and everyone wanted to win. But, George thought, those goals shouldn't come at the cost of abuse. A lot of people in the stands were men taking notes. They didn't care if the coach was a bully. They didn't care if any of these kids had hurt feelings. They were there on business.

So was George. He, too, was taking notes. He was watching the men in the stands as much as he was the basketball game. As a reporter for Sports Illustrated magazine, he was working on a story about an organization called the Amateur Athletic Union, or AAU. It was one of several organizations around the country that held games like this to scout young players who might have enough talent to play basketball in college and maybe, one day, for the Pistons, or Pacers, or some other team in the National Basketball Association. The other men taking notes in the stands were AAU scouts, coaches, and people from clothing companies that named their shoes after NBA stars. Those men hoped to find the next famous player, even if he was just a kid today.

The boy who missed the pass probably wasn't going to have a shoe named for him. He was thrown off the team for making one mistake, and George's heart broke

DOHRMANN FAMILY

At 10 years old, George Dohrmann caught a trout that was almost as big as he was.

as he watched him run to the locker room with tears in his eyes.

That boy was 9 years old.

Games like this, George later wrote in a book, weren't about sports. They were about business. Having fun and having feelings had no place in this business. Those things only got in the way of making money.

After the game, George asked the coach why he thought it was OK to use swear words with such young players. The coach said the boy needed to be "mentally tough."

George was glad he never had a coach like that when he was a boy.

Growing up in Stockton, California, George loved baseball, soccer, basketball, football … you name the game, and George loved it from the first time he picked up a ball.

But being good at a sport was harder for him than for most boys.

George was born blind in one eye.

Sometimes, he wore an eyepatch. He looked like a pirate. Other kids made fun of him. They called him "Popeye."

That was mean, but it didn't stop George from playing sports, even though he also was smaller than most of his friends. He still had fun, and usually he played well.

When he wasn't playing sports, George was reading about them. He read about sports the way most kids eat cookies — he couldn't get enough. When he was 9, he would sit on his dad's bed in the mornings before school to talk about the stories in that day's newspaper. His dad, also named George, had graduated from Notre Dame, and was especially interested in the news from that university. So, young George was, too.

By the time he was 10, George was an expert about college mascots — the symbols and nicknames that teams use as colorful brands. One summer, George was at camp playing a game to see who could name the most college mascots. The counselor would say the name of the school, and the campers would shout out its mascot.

"Michigan!" the counselor would say.

"Wolverines," George would respond. And most often, it *was* George. Some boys got the easy answers, like "Washington?" "Huskies!" But some kids had never heard of some of the schools. George had.

"Murray State?"

"Racers!"

"Austin Peay?"

"Governors!"

George had read about all of them.

In 1987, when George was in middle school, the Fighting Irish of Notre Dame had an outstanding basketball player named David Rivers. He was also co-captain of the team. He played point guard, the ballhandling player in charge of setting up the plays, and passing the ball to the right person at just the right time. George loved how Rivers could steal the ball almost any time he wanted, and to score almost any time he wanted, as if no one else was on the court.

So George copied his moves. He lined up at the free throw line just like Rivers. Before shooting, he palmed the ball — cradling it in his hand — and bent his knees just like Rivers. George had only one good eye, but he could still see who was best at teaching him what he wanted to learn.

As George got older, the balls got faster, especially baseballs. George had a hard time adjusting to the speed of the ball coming out of the pitcher's hand. One eye wasn't good enough to see the ball as well as really good batters had to do. So, George walked away from that game to spend more time playing basketball and football, as a defensive back.

Just because he would never be another David Rivers didn't mean he couldn't have fun. His joy for playing and his competitive nature helped him to be a better football player than a small, one-eyed kid had any right to be.

But as the football competition got bigger and stronger, so did the risk of injuring his good eye. So in high school, George stopped playing and found another way to stay involved in sports. He became a writer for the school newspaper, The Lincolnian, at Lincoln High School in Stockton. He wrote a sports column he called "The Jock Strip."

George was learning that you could have fun with words.

George, left, and his father, also named George, pose after young George's team, Off Campus Crime, won the interhall football championship at Notre Dame in 1994.

George was lucky to come from a family that could afford to send him on trips to look at colleges he might want to attend after graduating from high school. As a graduate of Notre Dame, his father, of course, hoped he would choose that university. His son certainly had the good grades to get in, and the school certainly had the sports tradition George would enjoy, but did it offer a way for him to combine them?

On his first visit to South Bend, Indiana, George fell in love.

Even in February, the Notre Dame campus was beautiful. The honey-colored stone buildings seemed to rise among the huge trees that by spring would wear lush, green leaves. The Golden Dome that gave residents the "Domer" nickname George had often heard his father use was topped by a statue of Mary, Mother of God. "Notre Dame" is French for "Our Lady," and she seemed like the beacon of a lighthouse showing George the way.

Then there was "Touchdown Jesus," the massive mural on the side of the library built when Father Hesburgh was president of the University.

Formally known as "The Word of Life," the mural's nickname comes from how it shows Jesus with his arms raised, like a football referee signaling a touchdown.

During his tour, George peeked into the office of The Observer, the student newspaper, where computers seemed to be waiting for him to start writing stories.

Practically within hours of arriving as a Notre Dame freshman, George went to The Observer in hopes of snagging a job as a reporter. He was surprised that such a well-known university had such a small newspaper staff. Even more surprising was that sports got very little coverage in the paper.

This was his chance to make a mark. He would make up for the lack of staff by doing the work of five reporters.

Every year, Notre Dame holds a boxing competition called the Bengal Bouts. It was a fun series of boxing matches, but the event didn't get much attention until the finals, when crowds would gather.

George thought people would be more interested if they knew something about each boxer. So, he spent time talking to them, finding out details of their lives that made them more like characters in a story than just guys punching each other in a boxing ring. With each story he wrote, more people read them in The Observer. And more people started watching the early Bengal Bouts.

Finally, The Observer published a whole special section about the Bengal Bouts. By the time he graduated in 1995 with a degree in American studies, George was recognized widely for making the bouts popular.

Because Notre Dame is so famous in college sports, the Fighting Irish get a lot of attention from what's known as the sports establishment — the businesses, athletes, media, and sponsors that make games nationally known. So George, as an Observer sports reporter,

DOHRMANN FAMILY

George, left, and his family — mother Suzette, father George, brother Greg, and sister Erika — celebrate his graduation from Notre Dame in 1995.

got to meet them all. He sat in the press box with people writing for national publications, he interviewed coaches, players, and professional scouts. He traveled with Notre Dame's teams to other universities and wrote stories no one else had thought of.

Today, George says of his college writing career, "It was an incredible training ground for journalism. Other colleges were not the same, not as deep."

After graduation, George got a job as an intern at the San Diego Union-Tribune newspaper. Then he got a better job as an intern and part-time writer at the Los Angeles Times. It published one of the best sports sections in the country, and George knew he was lucky to be there.

He learned the big-time newspaper business from the ground up. He got facts for other writers, he answered phone calls, he wrote about high school sports. He was the low man on the totem pole, but he drank it up like a man dying of thirst.

While writing about a local high school basketball star with strong potential as a future NBA player, George would wait to interview him when the bus dropped him off at school. One day, the player arrived not by bus, but in a new car he was driving.

Curious George wondered why. He looked up the license plate number on official records. He found out that the player owned the car. But the paperwork for the purchase was very odd. George wondered if somebody was trying to hide something. The car's previous owner was the UCLA basketball coach, and the player recently had agreed to play basketball at UCLA after he graduated from high school. So, it looked like he had been bribed with a car to play for that school.

The L.A. Times ran George's story. As a result, a lot of people asked a lot of questions, and the coach lost his job at UCLA. The school said he was fired for a different reason, not because of the story.

George was 24 years old.

At The Times, George became friends with a young editor named Emilio Garcia-Ruiz. Emilio liked to investigate stories about the darker side of sports. He liked to report about people who weren't playing fair. Emilio and George both disliked injustice and cheaters. They liked to expose the bad guys.

In 1997, when Emilio accepted a job as sports editor of the St. Paul Pioneer Press in Minnesota, he invited George to join his staff. It was George's first full-time job as a sports writer. At the L.A. Times, George was a small fish in a big pond; at the Pioneer Press, he would be a bigger fish in a medium pond.

In the spring of 1997, the University of Minnesota men's basketball team had made it to the Final Four of the National Collegiate Athletic Association (NCAA) tournament. It's one of the most popular sports events on any level — college or the pros. Any Final Four team is held in high esteem, and Minnesota had beaten UCLA to get there.

George and Emilio thought that was fishy. The Gophers — the mascot of Minnesota — didn't have the same winning basketball tradition as the other top-level teams with well-known student-athletes, like UCLA. Minnesota's success seemed to come out of nowhere. Were they cutting corners in class? George and Emilio wondered if, somehow, they had cheated. The next season, George covered the team for the paper. He developed sources at Minnesota, and began sniffing around.

He got the name and phone number of a former employee at Minnesota who now had a job with a small church in Wisconsin. He started contacting her to find out what she knew.

"I would drive to the little town where she lived," he recalled recently, "... and we would go to a coffee shop... I did this over and over again, hours and hours, weeks and weeks, months and months of trying. I don't smoke, but I would light up a cigarette and smoke one while she did, and try to get her to tell me more. Little by little, she did."

She told George that the university had paid her to write papers and take exams for players on the basketball team. Their names would be on the papers, but she had written them so that they would have good enough grades to keep playing ball.

Like the sketchy situation with the coach and the car at UCLA, that's a violation of NCAA rules. It's a violation of Minnesota rules, and a violation of common decency. George wanted to expose the cheaters. But his source was nervous. She didn't want to ruin her reputation, but she knew what they had done was wrong. She talked to George, but only off the record — that means she gave him information, but only if he promised not to say where he got it.

In journalism, it's common to collect information "on background," which means you have unnamed sources who give you a general sense of a story and who is involved. But when you write, you must include facts, and in most situations, you must say where you got them. Otherwise, readers wonder how you know what you claim to know. George knew he had a big story, but he also knew readers would not want to believe it unless he could prove it.

Finally, his source agreed to be named in his stories. Finally, George could prove what he knew. In March 1999, the Pioneer Press ran a series of stories about academic fraud in the Minnesota men's basketball program with George as the lead reporter.

It was such a blockbuster tale of corruption in college sports that George won the 2000 Pulitzer Prize for beat reporting. The Pulitzer is the highest honor a journalist can have in the U.S.

People who believe in fair play were glad the cheaters got caught, but not everybody was happy. A lot of Minnesota fans and Pioneer Press readers were angry at the paper and its writers. They didn't feel happy to know the truth, they felt betrayed. The woman who was George's main source also suffered. She lost valued friends. But as hard as it was, she was never sorry that she told the truth.

Sometimes, the truth is hard to live with. But it is a journalist's job to write the truth, no matter how painful it can be.

Only five sports writers have won Pulitzer Prizes, which have been awarded for more than 100 years. George Dohrmann was the most recent sportswriter to win, and the second one was Red Smith — he also went to Notre Dame, and his story, too, is told in Chapter 3.

As a Sports Illustrated writer sitting in a small gym that day, watching little kids being "coached" for basketball careers in college and beyond, George followed the AAU programs for eight years. Then he wrote his story of abuse and exploitation — the poor treatment of young kids just so that adults could cash in on their fame later. He wrote about kids being promised cars, shoes, and money, promises that never would be kept. He wrote about seeing kids tossed out of the program as if they were litter.

He turned the story into a book, "Playing Their Hearts Out: A Coach, His Star Recruit, and the Youth Basketball Machine." Like the story about cheating at the University of Minnesota, this one also won a major award — the 2011 PEN/ESPN Award for Literary Sports Writing.

Today, George is married, and he has two kids. He coaches youngsters at the YMCA, and supports their desire to play sports just because they have fun. He teaches writing at Southern Oregon University, and he still writes books about sports. His latest is "Superfans: Into the Heart of Obsessive Sports Fandom." He also works as an editor for The Athletic, an online publication. Its motto is "Fall in love with the sports page again."

THE AGENT OF CHANGE

Tommy Hawkins

In a lot of ways, Tommy Hawkins was a lucky kid. He was smart. He was good-looking. He was tall, and such a good athlete he could almost jump over the moon.

If Tommy had so much going for him, why were his knees knocking in fear? Why did he want to run and hide from people who just wanted to hear what he had to say?

"I can't do it," Tommy told the man he was with.

"Yes, you can. C'mon now," said Johnny Jordan. "It'll only take a couple of minutes — just tell them, let's see, just tell them why you came to Notre Dame."

Tommy Hawkins was new to the University of Notre Dame. He was a standout basketball player in high school, a player Notre Dame had wanted for its team. So after graduating from high school, Tommy became a member of the Fighting Irish, and both he and Notre Dame were happy.

He was 6 feet 5 inches tall. He could score and rebound at will in front of 4,000 fans at The Fieldhouse, where the Irish played on campus. But now, at a community event near the university, where he and Notre Dame basketball Coach Jordan had come, Tommy was so scared he wanted to hide in a closet. Why, he wondered, had he ever agreed to come with the coach, why had he agreed also to say a few words?

"I can't!" Tommy insisted.

Coach Jordan wasn't having any of it. He knew Tommy was more than a talented basketball player. Tommy was a sensitive young man whose background would be interesting and important for this audience. Coach knew that people like Tommy had lots to offer, if only they got the chance.

In 1955, Tommy was the first African-American player on Notre Dame's basketball team. He came from a family with little money, a family that didn't have many opportunities to make a better life. But that hadn't stopped Tommy from enjoying school, and getting good grades. It hadn't stopped him from learning about a lot of things about life, in addition to sports.

In Tommy, Coach Jordan saw a young guy who could

be a model student-athlete for the team, for the school, and for black people at a time in American history when such ideas were unusual in many places. He wanted to help Tommy go as far as he was able, and one way to do that was by helping him learn how to speak in public.

Coach Jordan introduced Tommy to the mostly white crowd. There was no way he could escape now, even though his knees were knocking so loud you could hear them up in Michigan.

So he spoke.

Guess what? He was terrible!

He stuttered. His voice cracked. He forgot what to say.

"I told you I couldn't do it," he told Coach Jordan. "Never again!"

"Next week," Coach said. "Again. We'll work on it."

Tommy Hawkins was born in Winston-Salem, North Carolina. He, his three brothers and sister, and his mom lived with his grandmother until they moved to Chicago, when Tommy was 6. Like other people with little money, they lived in what's called "the projects" — housing partly paid by the government for poor families. Public housing like this often was dangerous — there were gangs, drugs, and all kinds of crime that young boys often found tempting because it looked like the way out.

Tommy's mother, Juanita, who worked in a cafeteria, made sure he stayed closer to his schoolbooks than to troublemakers. When he was 10 years old, she told him about Jackie Robinson, who had just become the first black player in

HAWKINS FAMILY

Tommy Hawkins at 2 years old, with his baby sister, Eva.

major league baseball. She helped Tommy understand that when Robinson joined the Brooklyn Dodgers, it opened the door for other black people who hadn't been able to reach their dreams. Robinson was a symbol of what was possible for black people, for *Tommy*, in sports, and in any job or activity he wanted to follow.

By the time he was 12, Tommy was listening to his brothers' jazz records. He started collecting his own with the small allowance he got from his mom. The records were the old-fashioned kind that you play on a phonograph with a needle. He loved that music, the way it made him want to dance. The boy had moves! Jazz music became a part of his life that never left him.

He played basketball with other boys in the projects. They made their own hoops by using tall pieces of old lumber with old baskets tied to them. Tommy also loved baseball. He made his own balls from winding tape into the shape of a ball.

When he was 14, Tommy shared a locker at Parker High School with a white boy named Richard. They became friends. One day, an ugly fight started in the schoolyard. It was black kids against white kids. They were punching each other, and calling names.

Tommy said to Richard, "Do we have anything to do with that?" Richard shook his head, and they walked on.

The kids who were fighting yelled after them, and called *them* names. It was all about race — they didn't like it when a black kid and a white kid were friends. Tommy and Richard ignored them.

Back in school, they were called into the principal's office. What did we do, they wondered. Nothing bad, they found out. And everything good. The principal told them that they were excellent examples of how to behave in a world where mixing the races was new.

The principal was so impressed with how well they got along that he asked them to be ambassadors. They whispered to each other, "What's an ambassador?" An ambassador is someone who represents an idea or activity in positive ways. For Tommy and Richard, being ambassadors meant they were the kids at school who represented doing the right thing.

They were good at that responsibility. They talked with other students, and helped them see how silly, how mean, it was to fight over the color of someone's skin. For Tommy, that role would become second nature to him all his life. People would admire him for being smart, and playing basketball well, but they also would admire him for his character.

Tommy was a good student at Parker High School, and a great athlete. He was riding the train home from school one day, and reading the Chicago Daily News. A headline in the sports pages read, "Hawkins Leads City Preps in Scoring."

Tommy was amazed — he was only a kid in high school, and his name was in the newspaper! When he showed his mother, she gave him good advice — be proud, be humble, but act like you deserve it. He started to wonder — could a poor black kid like him go to college? People at Notre Dame thought he could — school officials invited him to visit. Of course, he accepted.

The campus looked nothing like busy Chicago, and the dangerous projects where he lived. Notre Dame was like a country estate you read about in storybooks. Tommy was a good enough student for Notre Dame, and a good enough basketball player to be offered a scholarship — Notre Dame wanted Tommy, and he wanted it.

In many cities, universities like Notre Dame often have clubs whose members once attended the school.

HAWKINS FAMILY

Tommy, bottom right, gathers with friends and family, including Grandma Hawkins, top left, and mother, Juanita, top right, in the 1950s.

They gather now and then for dinner and to meet high school graduates who would be attending their school in the fall. When Tommy was in high school, the Notre Dame Club of Chicago sponsored a father-son dinner for those local boys.

The Parker High School basketball coach, Ed

O'Farrell, asked Tommy if he was going to the dinner. "No," answered Tommy. "I don't know much about my father or where he is."

Of course, Coach O'Farrell knew that — he and Tommy were close. "No problem," he told Tommy. "I'll be your father!" Tommy happily agreed, even though no one would believe that he was the son of this white man. He smiled, and told his coach, "You'll have to work on your tan."

Tommy was the only black kid at that dinner, in the mid-1950s, and many years later in an ESPN radio interview, he remembered that the only other black people at the event were the waiters.

In the fall of 1955, he enrolled as a freshman. Tommy was thrilled to be there, but immediately he felt different — he was the only African-American in his class, and the first black athlete to get a scholarship to play for the Fighting Irish. In the mid-1950s, although things were changing in the world, Notre Dame was still a place where most faces were white. Through all four years of his college education, Tommy never had a class with another black student.

He adjusted to being "different" because most people treated him just like they treated everyone else. Some of the people he met at Notre Dame would have great impact on his life. It started with Coach Johnny Jordan, the man who made Tommy more scared than he ever had been by making him speak in public.

Coach Jordan steered Tommy to speaking lessons,

where he learned how to calm his nerves and say what he had to say. He used this tool the rest of his life.

Confidence also pushed Tommy into writing. One day, Professor Father Soleta stopped him on campus. "You need to give your writing some more attention," he suggested, according to an interview Tommy gave in 2012. "Why not take my class? I will make poetry live in your soul."

Poetry?

Sometimes poetry is hard to understand. But so is jazz. Tommy took the class.

On the first day of class, the professor read aloud the opening lines of "The Love Song of J. Alfred Prufrock," by his favorite poet, T. S. Eliot:

> Let us go, then, you and I,
> When the evening is spread out
>   against the sky …

The poem was entrancing. Tommy was floored by the words, by how you could rhyme "oyster shells" with "cheap hotels" to paint pictures. The poetry class made Tommy think about how words can communicate in many ways. How they can make you feel something you don't understand, and how that's OK.

There would be more magic in that class, and it made Tommy want to write almost as much as he wanted to play basketball. His other classes — history, psychology, literature — helped Tommy appreciate a lot of things that make life interesting. Basketball. Jazz. Poetry.

Father Theodore Hesburgh was president of the university when Tommy was there. He was one of the leaders of racial justice, not just at Notre Dame, but for the whole country.

Indiana, where Notre Dame is located in the town of South Bend, had a history of poor treatment of African-Americans — the Ku Klux Klan had a strong presence in the state. People who belong to the KKK believe that white Christians who are born in America are superior to everyone else, and deserve rights others don't.

During his freshman year, Tommy went to a pizza place in South Bend that lots of Notre Dame students liked. The owner, who didn't like black people, asked him if he had a reservation. That's like asking someone if they have a reservation at McDonald's. When Tommy said "No," he was told he couldn't be served.

At the time, Paul Hornung was a star quarterback for the Fighting Irish football team. He was famous and popular, and he liked pizza. He also was loyal to members of the Irish family. When he heard what happened to Tommy at the pizza parlor, he said Notre Dame students shouldn't go there until the owner apologized to Tommy and served him like everybody else.

In 2012, Tommy remembered that incident. He told a reporter, "Paul Hornung was a big man on campus with a lot of influence. He didn't have to get involved like that, but he did."

When Tommy was a sophomore — his first year on

the varsity team — the Irish were supposed to travel to Louisiana for a tournament. A lot of America was starting to accept blacks and whites living, working, and playing together. But some places, especially in the South, like Louisiana, were slower than others to see everyone as equal.

When the hotel manager where the team was supposed to stay found out that Notre Dame had a black player, he said Tommy would have to stay somewhere else, at a hotel for black people.

That was not going to happen. The Irish community, once again, came together in support of one of their own. Tommy's teammates voted not to play in the tournament — if the whole team couldn't stay at their hotel, no one would stay there.

Coach Jordan supported them. So did Father Hesburgh. In the interview in 2012, Tommy said, "I remember Father Hesburgh saying, 'Wherever a Notre Dame minority student isn't welcome, Notre Dame isn't welcome.' That was huge. He was such a great leader."

"I loved Father Hesburgh," Tommy later said in a radio interview shortly before he died. "He represented unconditional love, a passion for justice, and he took a personal interest in me.

"Johnny Jordan looked out for me. Father Hesburgh looked out for me. The whole school," Tommy said. Tommy and Father Hesburgh remained friends for the rest of their lives.

Tommy, starring for Notre Dame, shows some serious hops as he grabs a rebound in a tournament game against Kentucky.

By the time he graduated in 1959 with a degree in sociology, Tommy was one of Notre Dame's most memorable sports figures. He was Notre Dame's first black All-American. That is an honor voted by sports reporters from the Associated Press for students they judge to be among the best in basketball and football.

His remarkable jumping ability resulted in 1,318 rebounds during his college career. As of 2018, nearly 60 years later, it was the oldest standing school record in the history of Notre Dame basketball. When he graduated, Tommy was Notre Dame's top career scorer, with 1,820 points. And that was at a time when freshmen weren't allowed to play on varsity teams — those numbers are for Tommy's three years on the varsity team.

In 2004, he was named to Notre Dame's All-Century Team. He also was named to the Notre Dame Ring of Honor in 2015, which is bestowed by the Irish athletic department for contributions to the whole school as well as the basketball team.

Tommy became a professional basketball player, joining the Minneapolis Lakers of the NBA in the small forward position. The team moved to Los Angeles a couple years later. Although Tommy would play a few years for another NBA team, mostly he played for the Lakers, and he made Los Angeles his home.

After playing in the NBA, the college kid who once could barely talk to an audience in the South Bend suburb of Mishawaka, became a professional speaker. Tommy wanted to talk to school groups, business organizations, and charities. They wanted to hear him talk about Notre Dame, about sports, and race relations. About poetry, and jazz. They knew he was a man from a humble background who learned how to embrace the wonder life offers.

Tommy also had a new career as a radio and TV broadcaster. In 1987, he joined the Dodgers, working with another famous Tommy — Tommy Lasorda. He was the longtime manager of the baseball team that was the first to have a black player — Jackie Robinson, Tommy's first real sports hero. Now Tommy was working for the Dodgers, too, 40 years later.

He continued his love affairs with jazz — hosting a weekly radio program — and poetry. His book of poems, "Life's Reflections: Poetry For the People," includes one called "Jackie, Do They Know?" It's a tribute to the man who inspired Tommy as a 10-year-old — Jackie Robinson. Here a few lines:

> Do they know what you did
>   Jackie Robinson when you
>   broke that color line?
> Do they know the worlds that
>   you opened when the Dodgers
>   asked you to sign?
> Do they know the humiliation
>   that you suffered through
>   the years or how it felt to
>   stomach the threats and
>   constant racial jeers?

Tommy Hawkins died in 2017. He was 80 years old, and to the end he continued to be exactly what he wanted to be — the face of his race, and a man of the world. In a recent interview, his son, Kevin, said, "He loved Notre Dame with every fiber of his being. He said Notre Dame did so much for him, and grew him up to be the man he would become."

DOWN, BUT NEVER OUT

Rocky Bleier

Rocky Bleier charged through the jungle, a thick, wet, hot, and dark prison. There was no way out, it seemed, from a place where only poisonous spiders, snakes, and ankle-grabbing plants lived. Suddenly, he dropped flat and held his breath. He held his grenade launcher at the ready. Bees buzzed above his head and into the wide, tropical leaves.

But they weren't bees. They were bullets. Rocky Bleier was in the thick of the jungle in Vietnam, where the enemy was trying to kill him.

Gunfire crackled. Grenades exploded way too close. Rocky was fighting a war alongside his fellow soldiers, but where were they? He couldn't see anyone else. Were they even alive?

It was 1969, and only a year earlier, Rocky had been in a different kind of battle. People liked to call that kind of fight a "battle," but it was only football. It was only a game. *This* was a real war, and people died.

A year earlier, when Rocky was 22 years old, he was a star running back for the University of Notre Dame football team. Only a few months after that, he was a promising new Pittsburgh Steeler, excited to play in the National Football League. Success in the NFL was measured by how many points you scored. Success in this jungle was measured by the fact that you survived.

Suddenly, something flashed right next to Rocky, followed by searing pain on his left side. He had been shot! His leg was a bloody mess, and he could see only a huge gash where muscle and flesh used to be.

"I've been hit!" he cried out. A fellow soldier ran to him just as a grenade came flying toward them. It bounced off his buddy's chest and landed next to Rocky, ripping open his foot. The pain was unbearable. Rocky couldn't move. The jungle all around him burned.

A few other soldiers tried to drag him away, but they, too, were exhausted. Others were also wounded. Many were dead. Then, from out of nowhere, a burly soldier Rocky didn't recognize picked him up, slung him over

BLEIER FAMILY

In the late 1940s, before he was a star athlete, Rocky Bleier was a cowboy.

his shoulder, and carried him out of danger.

It took them six hours to go 1½ miles, but finally the weary men came upon a helicopter in a clearing. The soldier who had saved Rocky loaded him into the chopper, and off it flew, taking Rocky into a future he wasn't sure he would ever see.

He never knew the name of the man who had saved from the jungle inferno, and he never saw him again.

As an elementary school kid in Appleton, Wisconsin, Rocky and a friend of his shared a paper route. They delivered the Post-Crescent newspaper, throwing it from bags hanging from their bicycles. A delivery truck from the printing plant dropped the papers at the friend's house. They had to fold them just right so they could toss them onto somebody's porch as they rode past the houses. Not *near* the porch, but *on* the porch.

In winter, the newspaper route was more an adventure than a job. Rocky skidded over icy roads, dodging snowplows in the dark. But his customers could depend on him. He was a hard worker, like his mom and dad, who owned the local tavern, Bob Bleier's Bar, where they worked day and night.

The Bleier family lived above the bar. Rocky worked there, too, washing dishes and sorting empty beer bottles in the basement so they could be returned to the brewery. The bar was a block from St. Bernard's Catholic church, where, sometimes, Rocky was an altar boy at the 6:30 a.m. Mass.

For fun, Rocky went to play in Jones Park. Its steep, grassy slope was perfect for sliding down on a piece of cardboard. In winter, he went even faster on a sled over the snow.

Rocky's real name is Robert. He got the nickname

"Rocky" from his dad, who told people that even as baby, his son had muscles, and that he looked like a little rock.

He is the oldest of four kids in the family. Sometimes, Rocky, his sisters, and his brother walked to the Viking Theatre. They paid 25 cents to see scary movies, like "The Thing." Once, late at night, with Rocky and his brother in one bedroom and his sister sleeping in the next, Rocky growled into the wall between their rooms. "Slowly, the monster crept into her room," he said, scaring his sister wide awake.

As a boy, Rocky was bigger than other kids his age, and he had a lot of energy. He loved all sports, and played football, basketball, and baseball whenever he could. Rocky had more energy than there were sports to play, so he put some of it into music. In fourth grade, he learned to play the trumpet in the school band. On his way to school, you never knew if Rocky would be carrying a horn or a football.

In the sixth grade, Rocky had a knee problem. His bones were growing faster than his muscles. The problem was called Osgood-Schlatter disease, and it would heal by itself over time. But until that happened, doctors said Rocky couldn't run or play sports. They said it would take three years.

Three years! It was like a jail sentence. Just when all the other kids were getting into team sports and learning which ones they were best at, Rocky was sitting on the sideline, watching. But he was warned that if he

BLEIER FAMILY

Rocky was an all-state football player at Xavier High School, but he also excelled at other things, including basketball and playing the trumpet in the brass sextet (top row, wearing glasses).

BLEIER FAMILY

didn't take that break, he might end up with a limp, or in a wheelchair, and never be able to play the games he loved.

But Rocky was lucky. After sitting out of sports for all of seventh grade, his body started to heal. By the time he was 13, Rocky was running and jumping with the school basketball team. His dad bought him some weights and a bench, and even as a 13-year-old, he worked out hard with 110-pound barbells. He dreamed of being an all-star athlete one day.

Middle school wasn't the last time Rocky would have to put his sports dreams on hold. But now that he was back, now that he could dream, once again, of a football career, he was a little behind the other boys his age. When he was younger, he was big for his age, but now, he was a little smaller. He would have to make up in ability what he had lost in size.

Rocky was a star at Xavier High School. In football, he was chosen three times as an all-state running back. In the 1960s, it was more common for football players to play more than one position, and Rocky also played on defense. He was good at that, too — he was named an all-conference defensive back. A multisport athlete, Rocky was a team captain in football, basketball, and track.

Xavier won the state football championship, and Rocky's picture was on the cover of Parade, a national magazine, when he was named an All-American.

Even being a star high school football player wasn't enough for Rocky. He still played the trumpet, and the Xavier band was voted best high school band in the country by a national association of Catholic high schools.

When he was a senior, Rocky had to decide where he would go to college. He had never been to Notre Dame — he had never even been to Indiana — but he knew all about the university's famous football team. The Fighting Irish had been struggling the last few years, but the university had hired a new coach, Ara Parseghian, and hopes were high that the team could reclaim its glory. Rocky wondered if Notre Dame was the place for him.

His uncle took him to visit the school, and Rocky had never seen any place like it. The campus was beautiful, and the people were friendly. But it was as if something different was in the air. Somehow, it seemed to him, *everyone* there was special. Notre Dame was its own world, but just being there made him think he could conquer the world beyond.

Because Rocky was a good student and a standout football player, colleges and universities noticed him. About 20 colleges wrote him letters, inviting him to consider them as the place he would go to school and play football. One of them was Notre Dame.

Football officials invited Rocky back to the campus for an interview. At first, Rocky was thrilled. Then he noticed that they wanted him to come on the same day the Xavier band was giving a concert. It wasn't right for him to let the band members down, and he wanted to play his trumpet with them. Was his chance to go to Notre Dame lost because he couldn't be in two places at once?

The people at Notre Dame understood. One of the reasons they liked him was because he was good at a lot of things, so they set up the meeting for another time. And that was when he met Ara Parseghian. It was 1964, and by 1966, Coach Parseghian would take the Fighting Irish all the way to the national championship.

Many years later, Rocky still remembered the day he

UNIVERSITY OF NOTRE DAME

As a halfback in his second year at Notre Dame, Rocky got only one start, but still finished the season with the team's best rushing average.

met the coach. "Ara was overwhelming to me ... his piercing dark eyes. He *looked* like a head coach."

As a Notre Dame freshman in 1964, Rocky showed up for the first football drill — the 40-yard dash. He looked at his new teammates, and his eyes grew wide. These guys were monsters! he said to himself. What am *I* doing here?

Rocky wasn't really short — he was 5 feet 11 inches — but he was shorter than most of the guys who played high-level football. But, just like in high school, what he lacked in size he made up for in heart. He might not *be* big, but he *thought* big. Coach Parseghian liked that.

"A halfback," Rocky heard one of the coaches say, "is half tank and half cat." Rocky tried to live up to that description. He got only one start his sophomore year, but he ended the season with the team's best rushing average, or yards gained by running with the football.

The next year, the Fighting Irish were national champions.

After that season, 1966, Rocky's dad took him to an NFL game. The Green Bay Packers were playing the Pittsburgh Steelers at home, only 30 miles from the Bleier home in Appleton.

Rocky looked through the game program to see if there were any players as small as he was. He found one, a Steeler named Jim "Cannonball" Butler. When Rocky saw how fast Butler ran, it was all he needed to know. "That was the first time," he recalled in a recent interview, "I started thinking maybe I could play in the NFL."

In 1967, Rocky's senior year, he was named team captain. But he missed the last game of his college career because he hurt his knee and couldn't play. The team won that game, but Rocky was so upset at missing his farewell that he cried in the locker room. He cried different tears, tears of joy, when Coach Parseghian held up the game ball and asked the team, "What should we do with this?" The other players shouted, "Rocky! Rocky! Rocky!"

These days, sports is so important at many colleges and universities, and sports get so much attention, that some schools cheat in order to win. You can read about some universities that have done so in Chapter 7. Today, Rocky is still grateful that Notre Dame wasn't like that. "Luckily, for the student-athlete," he said, "there are still universities like Notre Dame and men like Ara Parseghian whose integrity is intact."

In 1968, Rocky graduated with a degree in business management. He was such a good football player that the Pittsburgh Steelers selected him to play in the NFL. That was the good news. The bad news was that Rocky got to play only a few games that season — he had been drafted into the Army!

Today, the U.S. relies only on volunteers to serve in the military. But in those days, young men also could be "conscripted," or told to serve in the military when the country needed additional troops. It was commonly known as being drafted.

In the late 1960s, the war in Vietnam deeply divided America. Thousands of servicemen were dying in its jungles and rice paddies, and many Americans did not believe the U.S. should be there. A few months after Rocky was drafted, he was lying, wounded in the jungle.

That grim day in 1969, the helicopter got Rocky safely out of the Vietnamese jungle and into the closest hospital. Rocky knew he was hurt badly, but he had to know: "Will I ever play football again?"

"No," the doctors answered.

The pain of seeing his dream fade was worse than the pain in his throbbing leg and foot. He would never play football again. He might never walk again. It was as if somebody slammed a wall down between him and the rest of his life.

As he lay in the hospital bed with a hole in his leg and his foot in shreds, Rocky vowed to prove the doctors wrong. I will *not* be crippled, he told himself. I *will* play football again.

Surgeons wanted to remove a toe on his foot, but Rocky knew he couldn't run without that toe. He said no. After many long and painful nights, he finally got out of bed, and started walking, slowly, with his smashed toe. As the wise saying goes, "The journey of a thousand miles begins with a single step."

For his bravery in battle, Rocky Bleier was awarded a Bronze Star and a Purple Heart.

After several surgeries to mend his wounds, after being hospitalized in Vietnam, and Japan, and Fort Riley, Kansas, one day, Rocky got a letter from Art Rooney, the owner of the Steelers. It said, "Rock — the team's not doing well. We need you."

Only three toes on his right foot worked properly. Still, he went to the track to work out. He fell down, doubled up in pain and tears. He kept trying, day after day. He lifted weights, and strapped them to his ankles to make his legs and feet stronger.

People told him that it wasn't worth it. They told him to forget football, to go get a job. But to Rocky, playing football *was* his job … or it should be. Exactly a year after he was wounded in Vietnam, Rocky showed up at the Steelers training camp.

He was skinny. Ever step he took hurt. He worked out with the team, but he was still far behind. He couldn't make a living playing football, so he sold insurance in Appleton. But by 1971, Rocky was back, on the Steelers' special teams — those players are on the field for kick-offs, punts, field goals and extra point kicks, and kick returns, as well as the units that try to block kicks.

By 1974, Rocky was part of the team's starting lineup.

Unbelievably, he ran faster than he ever had. Coaches were in awe. Players were in awe. How could someone who almost lost his leg run so fast?

And it was a team of very good players — the Pittsburgh Steelers won four Super Bowls between 1975 and 1980. Rocky's contributions were huge — in 1976, he ran for more than 1,000 yards. In 1979, he saved the Super Bowl win by recovering a kick in the last few seconds.

Rocky retired from football after the 1980 season. Today, as a financial adviser, he makes good use of his business degree from Notre Dame. His book, "Fighting Back: The Rocky Bleier Story," is all about his war experience, and how he fought back from serious injury. He donates his time to the Boy Scouts, Special Olympics, veterans groups, Habitat for Humanity, and many other organizations that make people's lives better.

From the time he was a kid, photos of Rocky have always captured the big smile on a guy with an even bigger heart.

FUN FIGHTING IRISH FACTS AND TALES

When Notre Dame was founded in 1842, its official name was "L'Université de Notre Dame du Lac." That's French for "Our Lady of the Lake," which refers to both geography and a Catholic saint.

What lake? Why French?

The land was 524 acres including two lakes, St. Joseph's and St. Mary's, but they were known by a single French name, St.-Marie-des-Lacs — St. Mary of the Lakes. The school's first president, Father Edward Sorin, also was French, and he named the school for the lakes in his native language

Why does a school with a French name founded by French missionaries have a leprechaun mascot and an Irish nickname?

In the mid-1800s, a terrible famine forced many people to leave Ireland. A lot of them came to America, and fought for the Union forces in the U.S. Civil War, from 1861 to 1865. One regiment of Irish soldiers was known for its bravery in battle, and "The Irish Brigade" suffered terrible losses.

In the early 20th century, the university's football teams were known for their never-say-die spirit, so the "Fighting Irish" nickname became widely known then as a salute to the brigade's courage and grit.

That's one version, anyway — the Irish are known for telling a good tale, and there are many other stories about how the school struggled with nicknames.

The Fathers of the Holy Cross gave Father Sorin $370 to start the university. Today, Notre Dame's financial resources are more than $11 billion.

Today, Ireland's population is about 4 million, and only about 1% of its people speak Irish, which is also known as Gaelic. Notre Dame began teaching Irish in 1868, and today Notre Dame students still can take Irish language courses.

"Notre Dame Victory March" is the university's fight song, notable for its opening line, "Cheer, cheer for old Notre Dame." It was written 100 years ago by two brothers who graduated from the university, Michael and John Shea. The song was first performed at Notre Dame on Easter

Sunday, 1909. In 1969, the 100th anniversary of college football, it was honored as the "greatest of all fight songs."

The leprechaun is a fairly new mascot at Notre Dame. Before 1965, when he (and it's always a he) was named official mascot, the university symbol was a dog — an Irish setter. The first one, who was born in the 1920s, was named Brick Top Shuan-Rhu, but after that, the dogs usually went by the same name — Clashmore Mike.

The Notre Dame band is the oldest university band in continual existence. It has been playing music since 1845. The marching band has appeared at every home football game since the sport started at the school in 1887.

Notre Dame's official colors are blue and gold. So why do so many fans wear green, and why does the football team occasionally wear green?

When the school was founded, blue and yellow were the chosen colors — blue for truth, yellow for light. After the Golden Dome and the Statue of Mary were gilded in precious metal in 1886, the official colors were changed, and yellow became gold.

Sometimes, the football team wears green jerseys. It is the head coach's decision, supposedly to inspire the team to play harder. There's little evidence that it works.

In April 1879, Notre Dame's Main Building burned down. It housed virtually the whole university, including the library and its 10,000 books. About 300 workers labored through the summer to rebuild the structure that stands today, topped by the famous dome and its statue of Mary, "Our Lady." The school's 324 students resumed classes in the fall of 1879, and today people associated with Notre Dame are known as "Domers."

The Notre Dame dome and statue have been regilded with gold 10 times, most recently in 2005. Gilding is a delicate process, and it must be done by hand. The cost of gilding the first time in 1886 was $2,000; in 2005, the cost was $300,000.

Like the 24-karat gold leaf that gives the Golden Dome its name, Notre Dame's football helmets are also the color gold, and they contain real flakes of gold.